Notes on English Literature

Chief Adviser: JOHN D. JUMP
Professor of English Literature in the
University of Manchester

General Editor: W. H. MASON
Lately Senior English Master, Manchester Grammar School

TO
THE LIGHTHOUSE
(VIRGINIA WOOLF)

W. A. DAVENPORT

Lecturer in English, Royal Holloway College,
University of London

BASIL BLACKWELL
OXFORD

ACKNOWLEDGEMENT

I should like to thank Mr. Leonard Woolf and the Hogarth Press for permission to quote freely from the writings of Virginia Woolf, and to thank Mr. Woolf for satisfying my curiosity about *Luriana Lurilee*.

First printed in 1969
631 97800 3

Printed in Great Britain by Alden & Mowbray Ltd
at the Alden Press, Oxford
and bound at the Kemp Hall Bindery

CONTENTS

GENERAL NOTE

This series of introductions to the great classics of English literature is designed primarily for the school, college, and university student, although it is hoped that they will be found helpful by a much larger audience. Three aims have been kept in mind:

(A) To give the reader the relevant information necessary for his fuller understanding of the work.

(B) To indicate the main areas of critical interest, to suggest suitable critical approaches, and to point out possible critical difficulties.

(C) To do this in as simple and lucid a manner as possible, avoiding technical jargon and giving a full explanation of any critical terms employed.

Each introduction contains questions on the text and suggestions for further reading. It should be emphasized that in no sense is any introduction to be considered as a substitute for the reader's own study, understanding, and appreciation of the work.

I. WHAT SORT OF NOVEL?

Introduction

Most of us, if asked of a novel we've been reading, 'What is it about?', would produce an answer in the style of the following summary of Arnold Bennett's *Riceyman Steps*:

> It is the story of a miser, a second-hand bookseller in Clerkenwell, who not only starves himself to death, but infects his wife with his passion for money and brings her also to an untimely end.

We would, that is, assume that the question could be answered by a summary of the plot with some indication of the characters involved. That such assumptions work much better for some novels than for others becomes obvious as soon as we try to apply them to *To the Light-house*, for, according to them, this novel is 'about' a middle-aged married couple, spending their holiday on the Isle of Skye with their children and friends, who discuss whether it will be possible to go to the lighthouse on the following day, disagree while sitting on the terrace and walking in the garden, have dinner and then agree that it won't be possible; after a passage of some years, during which the wife dies, the husband does go to the lighthouse with two of his children, and one of the friends of the family paints a picture which she had begun all those years before. Such a summary makes the book sound pointless, which I suppose some readers may feel it is, because it assumes that the heart of a book is in its events; it fails to give any idea of what the novel is like because it is applying to it standards which prove to be inappropriate.

'What is it about?' is not the only question one can ask concerning a novel, nor is it necessarily the most useful one, and I use it simply as a reminder that the word 'novel' is applied to books which are very different from one another, even in something apparently as basic as plot. Virginia Woolf herself remarked in her diary:

> I have an idea that I will invent a new name for my books to supplant 'novel'. A new — by Virginia Woolf. But what? Elegy?

and she actually called *Orlando* 'a biography' though it is fictional. She was here expressing the fear that her books would be read and judged according to a predetermined set of expectations as to what a novel should consist of— expectations, for example, that a story would be unfolded in a series of actions, scenes and conversations which both moved the story to a climax and gave clear portraits of the characters. Her fear was quite justified. Some critics have accused her books, especially *The Waves* (which consists entirely of the thoughts of six characters woven together in a framework of description of sea and sky) of not being novels at all; they have been called 'prose-poems' and 'essay-novels'; they have been described as insubstantial, unconvincing, eccentric. All that these views boil down to is a recognition that her novels are 'different', which, since this is what she was trying to make them, is not necessarily uncomplimentary.

Useful discussion of *To the Lighthouse* must begin from an acceptance of the sort of novel it is. One must, as it were, tune in on the right wavelength; otherwise interference will constantly blur what the novelist is saying. The speed with which one makes this attunement will depend on one's experience of novels and one's width of reading. Some readers will at first be puzzled by the absence of traditional landmarks, the complicated plot and the gallery of characters of Dickens, for example, or the clearly developing and consistently presented story of Jane Austen. Those who have read Sterne's *Tristram Shandy*, on the other hand, will recognize that it is no new thing for a novelist to abandon plot and to follow the rambling thoughts of his characters and will be the readier to accept Virginia Woolf's manner of proceeding. In some ways it is easier for us nowadays to understand her technique, because the plays of Beckett and others have accustomed us to significance without action, the development of film and television to the quick succession of images, and changes in the novel itself to a wide variety of ways of exploring the human consciousness. In spite of these things, however, some people still find Virginia Woolf a difficult author. Because of this I want in this opening section to consider some of the questions that *To the Lighthouse* raises—such questions as 'What sort of novel is it?', 'What did Virginia Woolf put in place of plot?', 'What is there to hold the reader's interest if suspense and variety of action are abandoned?' and so on. I shall attempt to suggest answers to these questions by examining some of the features of the novel and showing how Virginia Woolf makes it clear to the reader what she is doing. But before doing this I want to look at some of Virginia Woolf's critical writings about the novel, partly because her ideas are more quickly understood when they are being explained rather than being put into action, and partly because in her writings about theory we can see not only what she was trying to do but also why she was doing it.

Virginia Woolf's Ideas about the Novel

During the years she spent as a reviewer for the *Times Literary Supplement* Virginia Woolf found many opportunities, both there and in other magazines, to express her interest and pleasure in the work of novelists of the past. She was not rejecting them when she began, after her first two books, to express dissatisfaction with the conventional form of the novel. In her important essay *Mr. Bennett and Mrs. Brown* (1924) she agreed with Arnold Bennett, that novelists of all ages were doing basically the same things—writing about human character and attempting to create in fictional terms a sense of the reality and truth of the life their characters lived. Her quarrel with Bennett was about the particular means by which a novelist could represent these things. She felt that different generations of writers had to find their own way of best expressing what they meant; as she put it, 'the tools of one generation are useless for the next'. It was natural that her seeking a new set of conventions should be expressed in terms of criticism of the novelists immediately preceding her—Bennett, H. G. Wells and Galsworthy; these writers were producing their later work when she was beginning hers and were established authors who could be seen as setting the pattern which public taste expected in a serious novel. These Edwardian writers were to her 'materialists' who spent too much of their novels writing about material things: about clothes and houses, richness and poverty, masters and servants, social conditions and social gatherings—all aspects of outer appearance rather than inner nature. She thought that the novelist should be showing what his characters were, not what they wore.

She explained her dissatisfaction most clearly in the essay *Modern Fiction* (written in 1919). The conventional type of novel from which, as she said, 'life escapes', seemed to her a tyrannical master who must be overthrown:

> The writer seems constrained, not by his own free will but by some powerful and unscrupulous tyrant who has him in thrall, to provide a plot, to provide comedy, tragedy, love interest, and an air of probability embalming the whole so impeccable that if all his figures were to come to life they would find themselves dressed down to the last button of their coats in the fashion of the hour.

But, she said, 'Is life like this? Must novels be like this?' Her 'no' to the second question inevitably follows her 'no' to the first, since she believed that the novel must reflect life as it is and life is not to be contained in the organized plot in which some novelists tried to put it.

Her main objection is the failure of the Edwardian novelists to give a true picture of what human experience is like:

> Examine for a moment an ordinary mind on an ordinary day. The mind receives a myriad impressions—trivial, fantastic, evanescent, or engraved with the sharpness of steel. From all sides they come, an incessant shower of innumerable atoms.

These atoms, the fleeting mixture of sights, sounds, feelings and associations which make up each person's consciousness at any given moment, are what to Virginia Woolf novelists should be writing about:

> Let us record these atoms as they fall upon the mind in the order in which they fall, let us trace the pattern,

however disconnected and incoherent in appearance, which each sight or incident scores upon the consciousness.

It is this idea which led her to use what has often been called 'the stream of consciousness' technique. From her dissatisfaction with Bennett and the rest, and encouraged by the example of several other writers, notably James Joyce, she formed her own method of presenting character. This method, seen at its best in *Mrs. Dalloway* and *To the Lighthouse*, follows the quick shifts of idea and image which happen in everyone's mind, and shows what her characters are by means of these developing thoughts, rather than by invention of plot and scenes which might bring out their characters in a less intimate and less truthful way. Only through an exploration of the inner reactions of her characters could she hope to represent what life was to her, a mixture of opposites, an evanescent fusion of trivial and important, random and meaningful, transitory and enduring:

Life is not a series of gig-lamps symmetrically arranged; life is a luminous halo, a semi-transparent envelope surrounding us from the beginning of consciousness to the end. Is it not the task of the novelist to convey this varying, this unknown and uncircumscribed spirit . . .?

It is obvious that, if she wished to give such a sense of life in her books, she had to devise a much freer form of novel than the one she saw most of her contemporaries using. She did, however, realize that, though it was possible to write short stories or sketches which consisted entirely of 'myriad impressions', in the greater length of a novel it was difficult to stop this deteriorating into a formless and tedious collection of fragments. She knew that the writer must select from life in order to make the novel readable and to give it shape. We can see Virginia Woolf's recognition of this need in a review she wrote in 1919 of a novel called *The Tunnel* by Dorothy Richardson, a writer who had somewhat similar aims to Virginia Woolf's own. She described this novel, one of a series about a character called Miriam Henderson, as follows:

> The reader is not provided with a story; he is invited to embed himself in Miriam Henderson's consciousness, to register one after another, words, cries, shouts, notes of a violin, fragments of lectures, to follow these impressions as they flicker through Miriam's mind, waking incongruously other thoughts, and plaiting incessantly the many-coloured and innumerable threads of life.

Now this sounds remarkably like what Virginia Woolf said in *Modern Fiction* that the novelist should be doing but she finds that it does not work any better than the more conventional type of novel, because it presents only the surface of life, not the reality beneath. She agrees with the rejection of the old method but is not satisfied:

> We want to be rid of realism, to penetrate without its help to the regions beneath it and further require that Miss Richardson shall fashion this material into something which has the shapeliness of the old accepted forms.

She found, then, that the record of a character's impressions did not in itself produce a novel superior to a more conventional story; the material had to be given shape. In fact a novel has to have a 'plot' of some kind; Virginia

Woolf abandoned one sort—the chronicle of happenings, the births, marriages and deaths and the idea of hero, heroine, comic character and so on—but had to find something to take its place. Moreover this shaping spirit had to give to the novel the sense of the reality beneath the surface, for, as she said in *Phases of Fiction* (1929):

> . . . also we desire synthesis. The novel, it is agreed, can follow life; it can amass details. But can it also select? Can it symbolize? Can it give us an epitome as well as an inventory?

From these critical writings two main ideas thus emerge: first that the novelist must try to represent the moving current of life and the individual's consciousness of the fleeting moment, and secondly, that he must select from this current and organize it so that the novel may penetrate beneath the surface of reality and may give to the reader a sense of understanding and completeness. The first of these ideas explains why she used the 'stream of consciousness' method; the second explains why she never wrote a novel, not even *The Waves*, which used this method consistently throughout.

Narrative Method

When we turn from these essays to Virginia Woolf's novels, we can see how she moved from the conventional narrative of her first two novels, *The Voyage Out* and *Night and Day*, towards a more impressionistic style in her experimental *Jacob's Room*, a style which she perfected in *Mrs. Dalloway* and *To the Lighthouse*. These later novels abandon the use of a story, in the sense of a series of events, and concentrate on a small number of characters, whose nature and feelings are presented to us largely through interior monologue. It is in these monologues that we can best see Virginia Woolf's way of creating the sense of life she wanted, the 'atoms as they fall upon the mind', and it is her use of them that led to her novels being described as 'stream of consciousness' novels.

This phrase 'stream of consciousness' is no magic formula which immediately provides the key to an understanding of Virginia Woolf. It is necessary to remind ourselves that the phrase is no more than an attempt at a general classification of a number of novels which have concentrated on feeling rather than plot, and have presented feeling by creating an impression of the individual consciousness of their characters. Among the novelists who have been thus classed together there is considerable variation of narrative technique, since there are a number of ways in which an author can attempt to suggest the 'myriad impressions'. James Joyce in *Ulysses* used several different methods in various parts of the novel; here, for example, is a brief extract from a scene in a Dublin street:

> Done anyhow. Postal order stamp. Post office lower down. Walk now. Enough. Barney Kiernan's I promised to meet them. Dislike that job. House of mourning. Walk. Pat! Doesn't hear. Deaf beetle he is.

The thoughts of Leopold Bloom here are presented in direct speech but are split into fragments; the effect is of the mind making little jerks forward; we hear each separate little click of the machine though the brevity of each unit gives the impression of speed. Elsewhere in the long soliloquy of Molly Bloom at the end of the book, Joyce uses another technique:

You never know what old beggar at the door for a crust with his long story might be a tramp and put his foot in the way to prevent one shutting it like that picture of that hardened criminal he was called in Lloyds Weekly News 20 years in jail then he comes out and murders an old woman for her money imagine his poor wife or mother or whoever she is such a face you'd run miles away from. . . .

Here we again have dramatic monologue in that the thoughts are presented directly to us, but the impression here is of fluidity, the randomness of the mind, the way one thought overlaps another.

It is clear from these examples that the mind's processes can be represented in more than one way; the author simply chooses one method of selecting and arranging his material. Compared to these two the style of Virginia Woolf in *To the Lighthouse* is obviously less direct because she uses reported speech; it is also less interested in conveying the randomness of the mind. Consider the following extract (Mrs. Ramsay is measuring her stocking against James):

She looked up—what demon possessed him, her youngest, her cherished?—saw the room, saw the chairs, thought them fearfully shabby. Their entrails, as Andrew said the other day, were all over the floor; but then what was the point, she asked herself, of buying good chairs to let them spoil up here all through the winter when the house, with only one old woman to see to it, positively dripped with wet? Never mind; the rent was precisely twopence halfpenny; the children loved it; it did her husband good to be three thousand, or if she must be accurate, three hundred miles from his library and his lectures and his disciples; and there was room for visitors. Mats, camp beds, crazy ghosts of chairs and tables whose London life of service was done —they did well enough here; and a photograph or two, and books. Books, she thought, grew of themselves. She never had time to read them. Alas! even the books that had been given her, and inscribed by the hand of the poet himself: 'For her whose wishes must be obeyed' . . .'The happier Helen of our days'. . . disgraceful to say, she had never read them. And Croom on the Mind and Bates on the Savage Customs of Polynesia ('My dear, stand still,' she said)—neither of those could one send to the Lighthouse.

This passage is fluent and gives a clear impression of the way thoughts move on and branch out; the speed of mental action is also conveyed, since the references to James make it clear that these thoughts exist between one moment and the next. We have a sense too of the layers of the mind; one part of Mrs. Ramsay's mind is with the practical business of the present moment, while quite separate thoughts occupy the rest of her attention. But, though the passage flows on, it gives less of the effect of spontaneity than Joyce. The use of the third person and of conventional sentence structure gives less the impression of the impact of the immediate moment than of the process of reflection—the way memory and association are continually being called up. The passage is more distanced than that of Joyce; there is a greater sense of effect in the humour of Mrs. Ramsay's exaggeration and in the final sentence, and we are more conscious of the author's organization of the passage, which moves in an arc of thought from James, the stocking, the lighthouse back

again to the same things. This sense of organization is not
a disadvantage. The novel as a whole is reflective rather
than spontaneous, and the obvious selection by the author
focuses our attention on the *idea* of the working of the
mind, which (to me, at any rate) is more interesting than
a more naturalistic imitation of its confused processes.
The point that matters, though, is that, whether we call
what Virginia Woolf was doing 'stream of consciousness'
or something else, we still have to look closely to see what
her narrative technique actually consisted of, and in order
to bring out some of the characteristics of the narrative
technique of *To the Lighthouse*, I want to look first at the
opening sections.

The opening of a novel is often particularly indicative of
the author's interests and method, since here he is introducing his readers into an imagined world and is attempting to establish a relationship with us, not only by catching
our interest and giving necessary information, but also by
making us adjust ourselves to the kind of writing before us,
to its pace, its style, the things it is interested in.

To the Lighthouse begins by taking us into the middle of
a scene; Mrs. Ramsay's opening remark is the answer to an
unstated question, which we have to supply by picking up
clues from what follows. The reader's natural curiosity
thus becomes involved. We wonder who these people are,
what they are talking about and so on. As we read on,
prompted by this desire to know, we begin to recognize a
pattern in the narrative at the same time as we assimilate
names, facts, ideas. The pattern is one of brief statements
in direct speech separated by longer descriptions of the
characters' reactions and thoughts in indirect speech; we
are barely conscious of the author, for 'said Mrs. Ramsay'
slips unobtrusively into 'these words conveyed . . .', 'James

thought' and similar statements which belong to the readily accepted convention of the impersonal narrator. The unobtrusive quality and the novelist's care to make everything seem natural artfully conceal the fact that this opening is doing several things at once.

First the reader is being introduced to the characters and the world they occupy. The conversation about going to the lighthouse acts as a stone thrown into the middle of a pool; it starts ripples of reaction in the several characters, whose thoughts gradually spread wider to include all the details essential for the reader's understanding—the family, their holiday, their friends, the place in general terms and the immediate scene with mother and child sitting, Ramsay and Tansley walking, then Lily painting and so on. Since the facts are put before us through the thoughts of one of the characters, they come to us with associations of the character's personality, and so we begin to be involved in the tensions between them; we begin with the opposition of Mr. and Mrs. Ramsay, brought to us through the reactions of the sensitive child and with reference to the lighthouse, then move to the antagonism aroused by Tansley, the quarrelsomeness of the children, the impassive Carmichael; and so the strands grow in number and the texture of the book becomes complex as the novelist begins to weave them together.

Then, too, the pattern begins to establish itself, the pattern, that is, of conversation and reaction, of the actual words in the first person and the present tense, and the reflections of the characters in the third person and the past tense. The opening conversation consists of only eight short remarks of a normal, even trivial, kind, but from the beginning we are made aware that the surface of normal human relationships conceals a mass of tangled feelings and associations and that these feelings can be strong and passionate though they are concealed. This violence of feeling is seen first in the child, James, and seems natural to the exaggeration of childhood; we are thus prepared in an acceptable way for the emotions of the adult characters, tempered by age and experience, but made more complex too.

It is by means of this combination of the conversation that is actually happening and the connected thoughts that may range over any event, that a time-scheme is also established, in the sense of the present moment seen in relationship to the past, which is continually woven in with the present in the minds of most people.

The third-person narrator is, as I have said, a very common and easily accepted device. Virginia Woolf is, however, very careful to make her direction of the narrative as little noticed as possible. Her use of indirect speech for the interior monologues of her characters makes it easy for her to work into these mental soliloquies a number of statements and ideas which are outside the range of knowledge of the character she is dealing with. When, for example, at the beginning she describes the feelings of James about his father, she moves from what the child is thinking to what Mr. Ramsay habitually did and said, through impersonal sentences:

Had there been an axe handy, a poker, or any weapon that would have gashed a hole in his father's breast and killed him, there and then, James would have seized it. Such were the extremes of emotion that Mr. Ramsay excited in his children's breasts by his mere presence; standing . . . disillusioning his son and casting ridicule upon his wife, who was ten thousand times better in every way than he was (James thought), but also with some secret conceit at his own accuracy of judgment. What he said was true. It was always true. He was incapable of untruth; never tampered with a fact; never altered a disagreeable word to suit the pleasure or convenience of any mortal being, least of all of his own children, who, sprung from his loins, should be aware from childhood that life is difficult. . . .

The statements in the middle here ('What he said was true' and so on) clearly develop from what James is thinking, but we seem to move away from the child himself into a general comment, which, in turn, merges into the description of Mr. Ramsay's attitude towards life. Yet we hardly notice this shift because of the uniformity of style; the two currents of thought seem to flow together. Just as this third-person narration makes it possible for Virginia Woolf to move smoothly from one character to another, so in the novel as a whole it is a unifying principle; the central section *Time Passes* is different in its method, but the impersonal narrator can take over from the indirect speech of most of *The Window* without any immediate shift in style.

This detached but flexible style, which fuses narrative and description of thought, is one of the major ways in which Virginia Woolf gave coherence and form to her novel. I want, to end this section, briefly to point out some of the other important methods she used to fashion the material of her books and by which she attempted to suggest the reality beneath the surface.

She used, as most novelists before and since have done, a chronological framework for her novels, but she was not concentrating on a series of incidents, but rather on the idea of time itself and the effect it has on human life. In *Jacob's Room* and *The Waves* she uses the span of life from childhood to death; in *Orlando* and *The Years* a stretch of history. *Mrs. Dalloway* and *To the Lighthouse* are more concentrated, the former to one day and the latter to two days separated by a passage of years, but in both there is a strong sense of passing time. The central section of *To the Lighthouse* is called *Time Passes*, and the idea is present in the minds of several of the characters, both as they recall earlier years and as they consider the transience of the passing moment through which they are living. Chronology is for Virginia Woolf not only a framework but also a theme; she is concerned not to show a succession of events but to show the sense of the relentless march of time as an aspect of her characters' thoughts.

It is against the background of past and passing time that we see the reaction of Virginia Woolf's characters to the present moment. As we become accustomed to the novelist's exploration of the inner life of characters, we begin to understand that some moments are much more meaningful to individual characters than others; each moment that comes will shortly become the past, but before it goes it may become a moment of intense experience for someone. These moments may not coincide with any event at all, let alone a dramatic one, but may nevertheless be of supreme importance for a character's understanding of life:

> Let us not take it for granted that life exists more fully in what is commonly thought big than what is commonly thought small.

The use of such moments is another way by which shape and significance can be given to a novel, since they become

stable in a shifting world. In Part III of *To the Lighthouse*
Lily Briscoe remembers such a moment years before,
when Mrs. Ramsay had resolved the squabbling of Lily
and Tansley into

> this moment of friendship and liking—which survived
> after all these years, complete, so that she dipped into
> it to re-fashion her memory of him, and it stayed in the
> mind almost like a work of art.

This idea is intimately connected with Virginia Woolf's
search for 'epitome as well as inventory', for some symbol
of the nature of reality, around which she could shape her
novel. The reality could be found only by probing for the
meaning of life, and the shape of the novel by showing this
meaning in the life of her characters. The difficulty was, of
course, that the meaning of life is, at least for one who, like
Virginia Woolf, could find no easy answer in religious
faith, an open question: no clear answer could be given.
This difficulty Virginia Woolf turned to fictional advantage
by making her characters themselves into the questioners
of life:
'What does it mean? How do you explain it all?' asks
Lily in Part III, and
'What is the meaning of life?'
By introducing these questions into her imagined world,
the novelist has dramatized her own quest for a shape, so
that the resolution of her characters' doubts can become
the resolution also of her own artistic problem.
It is in the importance of the moment that Virginia
Woolf found one way of suggesting an answer to the
question, 'What is the meaning of life?', as is clear in
Lily's reply to herself:

The great revelation had never come. The great revelation perhaps never did come. Instead there were little daily miracles, illuminations, matches struck unexpectedly in the dark: here was one . . . Mrs. Ramsay saying 'Life stand still here'; Mrs. Ramsay making of the moment something permanent (as in another sphere Lily herself tried to make of the moment something permanent)—this was of the nature of a revelation.

The other main way of suggesting an answer is the use of imagery and symbolism. When in *Modern Fiction* Virginia Woolf tried to define life she instinctively used an image (the 'luminous halo') and elsewhere we frequently find the image of a globe or circle fulfilling the same function. In *To the Lighthouse* there are several important images and symbols, some of which I shall discuss in a later section, as also some of the ideas which I have mentioned only briefly here. But, even from this short summary, I think we can see how Virginia Woolf's ideas about the novel help us to understand why *To the Lighthouse* ends as it does—with a combination of the symbolism of the journey to the lighthouse, a moment of intense experience ('I have had my vision'), and the completion of a work of art; the novel and painting become identified and both have attempted to 'make of the moment something permanent'. As we become accustomed to the narrative method of the first part of *To the Lighthouse* (and also, though fewer characters are involved, of the third part), we begin to be able to form tentative answers to some of the questions which I mentioned earlier in this section. The author's concentration on weaving together the thoughts of her characters focuses our interest on the people, their natures, their feelings about one another. Through our interest in them, the tensions between them and the community which together they make up, we become involved in their preoccupations and their questioning of life. The novelist is creating a fiction which taps the reader's interest in fact—in what people are like and life is like—as well as his aesthetic pleasure in a work of art. He is being presented not with a story, but with an attempt to create the quality or texture of the life of certain imagined characters; through them Virginia Woolf can suggest some of the problems of life which all human beings face. She attempts to capture the 'feel' of life in her creation of her characters' reactions to the experiences of the moment, and also to test the 'shape' of life by introducing ideas and questions which make us consider its meaning. We are both involved and detached, alternately move into characters' minds and are made to stand back from them and consider what they are and what their life is.

Questions

1. Examine the composition of Section 10 of *The Window*. What are the characteristics of the narrative method here? What qualities of the passage would be lost if Mrs. Ramsay's thoughts were presented in the first person?

2. Why is it difficult to decide when Mrs. Ramsay's walk to the town with Charles Tansley took place? What reasons can you suggest for the way in which this scene is related to what precedes and follows?

3. What aspects of the effect of time on human lives are

shown in *The Window* in the thoughts of (a) William Bankes, (b) Mr. Ramsay, (c) Mrs. Ramsay?

4. Look closely at the use of the 'impersonal narrator's voice' in the first nine sections of *The Window*, and try to show what part it plays in Virginia Woolf's narrative method.

5. I have quoted from Part III Lily's reflections on the significance of moments of friendship and of revelation. At what points in Part I is the reader made conscious of this idea?

6. Those of you who have read a novel by one of the authors attacked by Virginia Woolf (if you haven't, Bennett's *The Card*, H. G. Wells's *Kipps* and *The History of Mr. Polly*, and Galsworthy's Forsyte novels are all entertaining books), will understand what she meant by 'materialist' novels. How would you defend such a book against her criticisms?

II. MATTER AND FORM

General

In my opening chapter I tried to show how knowledge of the author's intention could help us to see what sort of novel *To the Lighthouse* is. Such knowledge can prevent our reading it in the wrong way with false expectations, but it cannot, of course, determine our judgment of the novel, for what an author wants to do is not necessarily the same as what he succeeds in doing. It is for the individual reader to decide whether Virginia Woolf achieved a truer picture of life than the novelists she reacted against, and whether she presented a view of life which can give us a sense of the reality beneath the surface. I think she did, in the particular aspects of life she chose to treat, but some critics have based adverse opinions of her achievement on the very fact that her subject-matter is 'limited'—not just in dealing with only a small sector of society, but in the limitations of her liberal, intellectual viewpoint and of her view of human beings as isolated phantoms living a shadow-life in a hostile world. The success of a novel does not, however, depend on its inclusiveness or on the breadth of mind of its author; the narrow view can be a penetrating one as long as the artist has the skill to convince us of its possibility and to enable us, for a time, to share it.

Virginia Woolf was not only conscious of the limitations of her art but in some degree sought them, as we may see from some of the remarks she made in her diary; on 19th June 1923, for example, she said:

I daresay it's true, however, that I haven't that 'reality' gift. I insubstantise, wilfully to some extent, distrusting reality—its cheapness. But to get further. Have I the power of conveying the true reality? or do I write essays about myself?

She uses the word 'reality' in two senses here, as her inverted commas show: by the first she refers to her treatment of the external, 'materialist' aspects of life; by the second, the true, real nature of human life. This distinction would be clearer if we called the first type naturalism, the second realism, for, though these two words have often been used as synonyms, there is a need for discrimination either by keeping them apart in meaning or by inventing others for the purpose. Artists who are attempting to be true to life, in a real, inward sense ('realism') do not necessarily imitate the outward forms of everyday human behaviour ('naturalism'). Many novels which tell fantastic stories are deliberately written in a style which is close to normal conversation; Samuel Butler's *Erewhon*, Aldous Huxley's *Brave New World* and Orwell's *1984* are all novels of imaginary societies, with elements of science fiction and fantasy but their style is, for the most part, naturalistic. This combination of improbable incident and completely acceptable and everyday form and language had been made in English as early as Chaucer, who often makes the reader swallow incredible happenings by focusing his attention on the completely credible feelings of the narrator, and it has had a continuous history in prose fiction. The opposite combination of truth to human feeling expressed in stylized language, and in patterned literary form, obviously far from everyday expression, is one more usually associated with poetry or poetic drama—which is one reason why Virginia Woolf's novels have often been called poetic.

Her belief that the novelist should be concerned with creating an impression of life made her a realist, that is a writer who was trying to be true to the real experience of living; her belief in the necessity for form and symbolism in a novel made her select and arrange her material in a way which is non-naturalistic, that is different from the operations of ordinary life. One of the fascinations of Virginia Woolf's writing is to see the interplay of these two characteristics and the various forms it took in her later novels. The relationship of the two is the source of the tension which underlies and binds together her fiction. The tension can be seen in *To the Lighthouse* in many different terms: in the conflict between the flow of time and the individual consciousness of moments of revelation: in the relationship of the formless fragments of experience to the artist's attempts to create a sense of form; in the struggle between Mrs. Ramsay's conviction that in life there is no reason, no order, no justice, and her perception of its beauty and her love for people and happy relationships between them. This tension is one of the things I want to explore in this chapter, by examining the material from which the novel grew and some aspects of its form.

Our knowledge of the novel's source comes from Virginia Woolf's own description of the idea and subject-matter of the book, in her diary; on 14th May 1925 she wrote:

I'm now all on the strain with desire to stop journalism and get on to *To the Lighthouse*. This is going to be fairly short; to have father's character done complete in it; and mother's; and St. Ives; and childhood; and all the usual things I try to put in—life, death, etc. But the centre is father's character, sitting in a boat, reciting 'We perished, each alone,' while he crushes a dying mackerel.

Her idea of the book changed later to some extent, as she began to invent characters and to turn into fiction her own memories of her mother and father, and childhood holidays, and to develop her own fictional interests—'life, death, etc.'—but the roots of the novel in her own life remained, as we can see from the remarks she made two years after the book's completion:

Wednesday, November 28th (1928)
Father's birthday. He would have been 96, 96, yes, today; and could have been 96 . . . but mercifully was not. His life would have entirely ended mine. . . . I used to think of him and mother daily; but writing the *Lighthouse* laid them in my mind. . . . (I believe this to be true—that I was obsessed by them both, unhealthily; and writing of them was a necessary act.)

We cannot, of course, read *To the Lighthouse* as an autobiographical novel, for Virginia Woolf turned her mother and father into Mr. and Mrs. Ramsay and included herself only in the concerns of the artist, which are part of the character of Lily Briscoe. Nor is this knowledge of the origin of the work necessary to our understanding of the book, but it does provide several pointers which may lead the reader to realize more quickly, why the book is as it is. The importance of time, for example, and the gap of years in the middle of the book, relate easily to the origin of the novel in the author's looking back across the years to her own childhood. Looking back, sometimes with a nostalgia which Virginia Woolf feared might make the novel seem sentimental, may have led to the reflective quality which I have already noted in the third-person narrative of the characters' thoughts. That the scene and action of *The Window* is partly a creation of an imagined picture and partly a recreation of a picture existing for years in the author's memory helps us to understand how Virginia Woolf managed to convey to us so convincingly the ambiguities of her characters' existence—the mingling of past and present time in their thoughts, for instance, and the way that life is shown being lived and, at the same time, observed.

The distinction between fiction and autobiography, which we can observe in many novels (D. H. Lawrence's *Sons and Lovers* for example) is even clearer than usual in *To the Lighthouse*, for Virginia Woolf did not recreate what actually happened in her childhood, nor attempt to dramatize her own relationship with her parents. The novel is an evocation of the contradictions of personality and an evaluation of attitudes of mind, which may have started from her own experience, but which developed into a questioning of the nature of reality and the role of her own art. She wished to create a true sense of the life experienced by her characters but also to give a sense of order and completeness to her fiction. This sense of order, whether we see it as synthesis, epitome, symbolism or whatever, involved selection, the imposition of shape on experience. We can see how the reality and the pattern grow together by looking at part of *The Window*.

In the first three sections of the book, the picture given of the Ramsay family and their friends is a fairly simple one; there is an everyday scene, a normal conversation and so on. But there are undercurrents, presented in the feelings of James and Mrs. Ramsay's reactions to Tansley, which introduce the ideas of inconstancy of feeling and the different impressions people make on each other. The fourth section moves to the thoughts of Lily and Bankes, who, on this first appearance, stand apart from the others and think about them. Their role as observers or commentators is made clear in Lily's attempt to represent the scene in her picture, and in her expression of the difficulty of judging people. These four sections present all the material from which the rest of *The Window* is developed: the people, the scene, the observers, the idea of the lighthouse journey, the difficulty of knowing people and of summing them up, the problems of the artist, the movement of time. We are shown the area of life which we are to explore and our attention is focused on the idea of seeing and attempting to understand.

The introduction of an artist into her novel provides a character who can be involved in the action and yet stands outside it because her work leads her to consider the nature of what she observes. Placing Lily with her easel, looking from the lawn to the house, also seems to give a special significance to the group by the window, who form the centre of the first part of the book. This scene is constantly kept before us; the characters' thoughts may wander into the past or away from their immediate surroundings but any action outside the present scene is subordinated to it. So Tansley's walk into the town with Mrs. Ramsay is developed from and returns to her thoughts about him as she sits there, and later the expedition to the beach is narrated in brackets, between a question from Mrs. Ramsay and Prue's immediate answer; the novelist gives a signal to show that we are not really leaving the scene but merely glancing aside for a moment.

Keeping the scene before us is one of the ways in which Virginia Woolf links together the separate characters and their individual thoughts. They are given a framework with which they are all involved and which is the source of their reflections. The interior monologues are seldom of such length that the place and the present moment can be forgotten, and the longer ones include images or ideas which relate back to the house and the garden. Look, for example, at the presentation of Mr. Ramsay's thoughts in Section 6 and notice how reference to his wife and child at the window, the pipe in his hand and the urn of geraniums relate what he thinks to his surroundings.

The first four sections also act as a pattern for the development of the material presented to us. A fuller exploration of the fluctuating feelings of Mrs. Ramsay, of the relationship of husband and wife and of Ramsay's thoughts, is followed by a more involved treatment of Lily and Bankes. It is clear that the novel is not progressing forwards but inwards, showing us the same figures and ideas in gradually increasing depth and complexity. We are not made aware of how characters develop and change but how our sense of them changes as we know more about them. This growth in complexity is seen not only in the Ramsays, but the observers too are seen to be less detached than at first appeared. Bankes's old friendship with Ramsay, his love for Mrs. Ramsay and Lily's attachment to the whole family complicate their view. The difficulty of clear vision is again developed by reference to the painting and Lily's symbolic rendering of mother and child as a purple triangle—only in a symbol can the complexity of human beings be represented.

It is only after a further exploration of Mrs. Ramsay's thoughts as she sits alone that Virginia Woolf turns back to a simple view, by a deft shift of Lily's attitude, as she sees the Ramsays watching their children and thinks: 'So that is marriage.' The simplified view points out how far we have been taken from the opening conversation. We have now seen the contradictions in Mrs. Ramsay, whose fear of life is set against her involvement in it and her ability to create happiness for others, and in Mr. Ramsay, who no longer appears an eccentric, selfish, bad-tempered tyrant but a man in whom these qualities are mixed with tenderness and nobility of mind. People cannot be summed up simply; human relationships are complicated and human life is transient. These ideas have been rendered for us in the developing exploration of fictional characters.

The reader's sense of growing knowledge and complexity, and of developing ideas, is accompanied by a response to the sense of form in the narrative. In single monologues, describing her characters' thoughts, Virginia Woolf moves from the immediate scene, develops the reaction and returns to the point at which she began; in the development of the characters one aspect balances another, one mood complements another; the succession of the sections has a pattern of alternation in the movement from one set of characters to another, and in Part III from one scene to another. We can find the same characteristics in all three parts of the book and in the novel as a whole. *The Window* begins and ends with a conversation about the lighthouse, with the same characters involved; it is as if the end answered the beginning, or completed what it left unsettled. Even the particular details correspond since the doubt in Mrs. Ramsay's opening 'if it's fine tomorrow' is answered by her 'you were right. It's going to be wet tomorrow'. *Time Passes* progresses from night to day, from sleeping to waking in the same circling way, and *The Lighthouse* again creates a pattern of question and answer—Lily's opening, 'What does it mean then, what can it all mean?' corresponding to the final words of the novel, 'I have had my vision'. The novel as a whole completes a circle of thought too: the journey to the lighthouse, proposed at the beginning is achieved at the end. The sense of completion is there in the movement of the two outer sections from scenes of dissension at the beginning to moments of harmony and reconciliation at the end. The sense of pattern, often a pattern of alternation or of one movement answering another like the ebb and flow of the tide, is suggested in so many ways in the book that the reader comes to expect it, and to accept it as a method of organization which functions quite as effectively as a different type of novel's use of a developing story.

The 'story' of *To the Lighthouse* does not, in a sense, develop at all. When we return to the house in Part III Mrs. Ramsay is dead and the only change she can undergo is in Lily's understanding of her. Though Lily and Ramsay experience a moment of achievement at the end of the book there is no suggestion that they are permanently changed; they remain the people they were at the beginning of the book. Even with James, who does develop in adult judgment, Virginia Woolf does not give us any reason to think that the mixture of enmity and admiration in his attitude to his father will alter. All the sense of change and development is in the workings of time and in our under-standing of the characters and their lives; an understanding which sees their individual response to the conflict

C

Virginia Woolf saw in life—the tension between what is temporary, unstable and mortal and what remains.

The situation of the artist is representative of the general human one, and by focusing on the idea of the permanence of art and the transience of life, as she does in Lily's reflections, Virginia Woolf establishes a standard by which the lives of the rest may be placed. Lily, imagining Carmichael's answer to her question 'How do you explain it all?', thinks:

> That would have been his answer, presumably—how 'you' and 'I' and 'she' pass and vanish; nothing stays; all changes; but not words, not paint.

The individual endeavour to 'make of the moment something permanent' has force in the novel because *To the Lighthouse* includes a treatment of the passage of time. The achievement of Mrs. Ramsay seems all the greater, against this background, for she has been able to say 'Life, stand still here' and has created the sense of permanence from the intangible materials of human relationships.

It seems to me that Virginia Woolf's achievement as a novelist can be seen in the same way; she too deals in intangibles, the most indefinite aspects of human feeling, but can, by her powerful sense of form, create symbols of the mind's attempts to understand and combat the chaos of life. This quality of her work is summed up in the remark E. M. Forster made in *Two Cheers for Democracy*, in a moving tribute to her achievement:

> . . . sometimes it is as a row of little silver cups that I see her work gleaming. 'These trophies,' the inscription runs, 'were won by the mind from matter, its enemy and its friend'.

Time Passes

It is in Part II of the novel, *Time Passes*, that the ideas of transience and the chaos of life are most fully developed, and since this is, in some ways, a difficult section, I want to discuss it more fully than Parts I and III. Virginia Woolf herself was anxious about the reception of *Time Passes*, and thought people might find it odd or difficult. She described it in her diary as 'the most difficult abstract piece of writing' and 'this impersonal thing . . . the flight of time and the consequent break of unity in my design'. But its place in the novel is easy to justify and, though some critics have disliked it and thought it too high-flown, it seems to me a fine example of rhetorical prose.

The section begins with the most conventional and uncommunicative passage in the whole novel, a brief conversation with no comment other than description of the actions of Andrew, Prue, Lily and Bankes as they come in from their late-night walk. Here Virginia Woolf is both linking the section to what has gone before and providing a normal, easily understood opening to her passage of abstraction, but she also shows by her laconic presentation of the scene that she is turning away from the individuality of her characters. The conversation looks forward in its opening remark, 'We must wait for the future to show', which, even while it brings the day to an end, anticipates the quick succession of years which is to follow. Unity with the rest of the book is visible also at the end when Lily's waking leads naturally into the events of the day.

With a span from bed-time to waking, the section is unified with the others in time, in that it is night between two days. The fact that between sleeping and waking not

one but many nights have passed is made acceptable to
the reader by development from the first night's darkness,
which obliterates the identity of people and things, to the
idea of the distinctness of separate nights themselves
being lost:

> But what after all is one night? . . . Night succeeds to
> night.

The nights, days and years are fused together and the
effacing darkness becomes the erasing quality of time
itself, which sets to work on the empty house:

> The house was left; the house was deserted. It was left
> like a shell on a sandhill to fill with dry salt grains now
> that life had left it. The long night seemed to have set in.

During this long night the people of the earlier narrative
seem to take on the quality of dream figures, seen from a
distance and seen only fragmentarily. Virginia Woolf is
herself wiping out the identity of her characters, as she
shows the eternal forces at work in opposition to human
society: time and nature break up the community and
begin to erode the house, the empty shell which once they
inhabited. This explains why the lives of the characters are
here dealt with so summarily: the death of Mrs. Ramsay,
which is, in one way, the central event of the book, the
marriage and death of Prue, the death of Andrew, are
conveyed briefly in brackets as if they were mere inci-
dentals. Careful reading makes it clear that these events
are seen here as illustrations of universal patterns, rather
than having significance in themselves. Hence the marriage
of Prue is presented as a single manifestation of the
universal cycle of the seasons, and her death of the

a force working; something not highly conscious[...]
thing that leered, something that lurched; som[...]
inspired to go about its work with digni[...]
solemn chanting. Mrs. McNab groar[...]
creaked.

This passage shows also how the t[...]
as generalized figures, flat char[...]
section as a whole. They ar[...]
midwives:

> ... some rusty labor[...]
> as the women, [...]
> slapped and s[...]
> cellars. Oh, they[...]

This birth brings the r[...]
people return; the long ni[...]
up a community is again a[...]
individual human life to contin[...]

The Three-part Structure

To the Lighthouse is the only one of Vir[...]
novels which is divided into separate parts, eac[...]
has a title. Her first novels were written in conv[...]
chapters and the others either continuously with no b[...]
or in sections marked by a gap or a number, as, within [...]
parts, *To the Lighthouse* is. Her diary shows that the triple
arrangement was in her mind almost from the first idea she
had of the book. She described it as 'father and mother
and child in the garden; the death; the sail to the lighthouse', and again: 'I conceive the book in 3 parts. 1. at the
drawing room window; 2. seven years passed; 3. the

To the Lighthouse

inevitable sorrows of mankind. More significant for the
novel as a whole, the death of Mrs. Ramsay is dealt with
in a similar way:

> The nights now are full of wind and destruction; the
> trees plunge and bend and their leaves fly helter skelter
> until the lawn is plastered with them and they lie packed
> in gutters and choke rain pipes and scatter damp paths.
> Also the sea tosses itself and breaks itself, and should
> any sleeper fancying that he might find on the beach an
> answer to his doubts, a sharer of his solitude, throw off
> his bedclothes and go down by himself to walk on the
> sand, no image with semblance of serving and divine
> promptitude comes readily to hand bringing the night to
> order and making the world reflect the compass of the
> soul. The hand dwindles in his hand; the voice bellows
> in his ear. Almost it would appear that it is useless in
> such confusion to ask the night those questions as to
> what, and why, and wherefore, which tempt the
> sleeper from his bed to seek an answer.
>
> (Mr. Ramsay stumbling along a passage stretched his
> arms out one dark morning, but, Mrs. Ramsay having
> died rather suddenly the night before, he stretched his
> arms out. They remained empty.)

In this passage the event of death is deliberately distanced;
not only is it narrated in brackets but the syntax of the
sentence removes it further from direct impact upon the
reader, telling of the death not in a main clause or with a
finite verb at all, but in a 'participial absolute' construction
(if we have to give it a name), unrelated grammatically to
the rest of the sentence, and referring to the event retro-
spectively. Because of this distancing her death appears as

reflecting upon their quality. In *Time Passes* the novelist steps back from this circle of activity until it seems a mere speck in the perspective of eternity, but in *The Lighthouse* we are brought back to a mixture of action and reflection.

It is, however, the observation of life that seems most strongly emphasized. The two creative figures, Lily, the painter, and Carmichael, the poet, sit on the lawn in silent communication between the house and the sea. Lily turns from one to the other sending her thoughts back to Mrs. Ramsay as she looks at the house and outwards to Mr. Ramsay as she follows the course of the boat. She thus forms a tenuous thread between past and present, between husband and wife; by recreation of past experience and of the spirit of Mrs. Ramsay, and imaginative involvement with Mr. Ramsay's symbolic voyage, she unites the two in her mind, and so achieves her sense of completeness, of having seen it all clearly, if only for a moment. The two actions, the arrival at the lighthouse and the last stroke of the brush, are also united; both are acts of completion and it is obvious that they are meant to happen together, even without confirmation once again from the diary, where Virginia Woolf says:

> Could I do it in a parenthesis?—So that one had the sense of reading the two things at the same time?

Questions

1. How, other than by the direct recollections of Lily, is the reader made aware of Mrs. Ramsay in Part III of the novel?

2. Examine the parts of *Time Passes* which deal with the house and try to describe their effect.

---

thoug
and im
lack of pu
Ramsay. Bu
despair, turns
time and decay
activity. The house
the book moves forwa
establish some positive
remains?'

This analysis makes the s
solemn than it in fact is. Virgin
these universal questions with eco
graceful description, in which we see
stillness and innocence as well as its destr

> So loveliness reigned and stillness, and tog
> the shape of loveliness itself, a form from which
> parted; solitary, like a pool at evening, far distan
> from a train window, vanishing so quickly that
> pool, pale in the evening, is scarcely robbed of it
> solitude, though once seen.

The passage also employs deliberate anticlimax by which the tone of the prose is lowered; this is particularly so in the humorous passages describing Mrs. McNab and Mrs. Bast:

> If the feather had fallen, if it had tipped the scale downwards, the whole house would have plunged to the depths to lie upon the sands of oblivion. But there was

3. What design can you see in the sections of *The Lighthouse* other than the alternation of the scenes of the lawn and the boat?

4. Show the different ways in which Virginia Woolf makes the reader aware of the idea of 'life observed' in *To the Lighthouse*.

5. What different types of humour have you noticed in the novel? What is the function of irony in *To the Lighthouse*?

6. Why do you think D. H. Lawrence's *Sons and Lovers* seems more autobiographical than *To the Lighthouse*? Compare the use of painting in the two books.

III. CHARACTER AND PRESENTATION

Virginia Woolf's rendering of character has often been seen as a weak point in her work; contemporary reviewers accused her of failing to present convincing pictures of characters and even her admirers have sometimes criticized her in this respect. E. M. Forster, for example, wrote:

> She could seldom so portray a character that it was remembered afterwards on its own account, as Emma is remembered, for instance, or Dorothea Casaubon.

It is true that if one expects a novel to be a portrait gallery, to be full of Mr. Micawbers, Mr. Collinses and Squire Westerns, one will inevitably feel that Virginia Woolf's characters lack definition, are not 'rounded', are not in fact 'portraits' in the same sense at all. This is not equally true of all her novels for in her early book *Night and Day*, written before she moved away from the conventional type of novel, you will find a lively comedy of manners, embodying witty presentation of several amusing characters such as William Rodney and Mrs. Hilbery. But from this kind of novel she moved on, for reasons which I have explained in Chapter I, to novels which attempted to create a greater sense of life and of the way human beings really think and have their being. A presentation of people as they are, rather than as they would make good character-sketches, leads her to show us the variety of human emotion, the indefiniteness and fluidity of character. As one of Virginia Woolf's most sympathetic and perceptive critics, Joan Bennett, puts it:

46

She perceived the variety of impressions made by one person upon the people around him and his own ever-changing consciousness of the surrounding world. Consequently, instead of defining an identity or epitomizing it in a particular incident, she invites us to discover it by living in the minds of her characters . . .'

It is not possible to describe the characters of *To the Lighthouse* simply or concisely, precisely because the author has deliberately shown their indefinableness; she has chosen to create in fictional terms the sense that all of us have about our family and friends, that we know them too well to be able to have one unmixed reaction to them; we know their good and bad points but recognize that making a list of these still leaves out much of our feeling. Virginia Woolf has made sure that we realize how foolish simple assessments of people are, for *To the Lighthouse* is about the difficulty of summing them up:

How did one judge people, think of them? How did one add up this and that and conclude that it was liking one felt, or disliking?

reflects Lily, as she thinks about Bankes and Ramsay in Part I. This theme is developed fully in Part III where Lily, as she paints, remembers Mrs. Ramsay and tries to define her character. At one point she draws up a kind of balance sheet of her qualities, remembering that some people disliked her and found her stand-offish, too self-confident, weak with her husband and so on; then she thinks of her relationship with her husband, the conflict and the harmony, but she has already realized the impossibility of her task:

One wanted fifty pairs of eyes to see with, she reflected. Fifty pairs of eyes were not enough to get round that one woman with, she thought . . . one wanted most some secret sense, fine as air, with which to steal through keyholes and surround her where she sat knitting, talking, sitting silent in the window alone; which took to itself and treasured up like the air which held the smoke of the steamer, her thoughts, her imaginations, her desires.

It is not by the use of her reason that Lily is able to encompass Mrs. Ramsay, but only through the intuitive power of the artist. As a triangular shadow falls on the step, the scene of Part I with Mrs. Ramsay and James sitting at the window is recreated, and to Lily suddenly for a moment Mrs. Ramsay is there again. It is a moment of vision or of revelation which embraces Mr. Ramsay as well; Lily feels that she has given him the sympathy he had wanted. Something has been completed; for a moment of intense experience has given her an understanding, which is symbolically represented in the completion of her picture.

One of the main reasons for the difficulty of judging people Virginia Woolf saw in the inadequacy of human relationships. Human beings seemed to her isolated and communication between them partial, often unsatisfactory, sometimes quite mistaken. *To the Lighthouse* shows us various fictional characters, trying, with varying degrees of success, to establish relationships with the people around them.

One of the sources of failure is that the main means of communication is words; words often fail to express with exactness the complexity of human feelings and, in any

case, the words people use represent only a fraction of
what they actually think and may give quite a misleading
impression. Virginia Woolf has a keen penetration into
both these aspects of verbal inadequacy. As Lily stands
near to Carmichael on the lawn trying to explain Mrs.
Ramsay, she thinks:

> she wanted to say not one thing, but everything. Little
> words that broke up the thought and dismembered it
> said nothing. 'About life, about death; about Mrs.
> Ramsay'—no, she thought, one could say nothing to
> nobody. . . . Words fluttered sideways and struck the
> object too low. . . . For how could one express in words
> these emotions of the body?

She feels in greater communication with Carmichael
sitting there in silence than if they spoke and this is a
feeling she has already divined in Mrs. Ramsay:

> Mrs. Ramsay sat silent. She was glad, Lily thought, to
> rest in silence, uncommunicative; to rest in the extreme
> obscurity of human relationships. Who knows what we
> are, what we feel? . . . Aren't things spoilt then, Mrs.
> Ramsay may have asked (it seemed to have happened so
> often, this silence by her side) by saying them? Aren't we
> more expressive thus?

But Mrs. Ramsay is also a person who, except in her
pessimistic moments, tries to establish communication
between people, and Virginia Woolf shows this in many
ways: in Mrs. Ramsay's attitude to Paul and Minta and to
Lily and Bankes, for example, and at the dinner party
where, seeing the unease of her guests, she begins to make
the effort to get people talking, to involve them and so to
create something of the time they are together.

D

To the Lighthouse presents the reactions of people to one another in such a way as to create for us the ebb and flow of feelings, the movement of characters towards one another from the state of isolation in which each one of us is trapped by his own sense of inadequacy or his private worries. Tansley is a convincing picture of a man trapped in this way; sensitive, feeling socially inferior, badly dressed, unattractive, poor, he seeks to assert himself in compensation and so speaks aggressively, with rudeness and arrogance, making a bad impression on everyone except Ramsay, with whom his intellectual ability creates communication, and Mrs. Ramsay. Her feelings about him vary, but she is pictured as the rare person who can make others show their best side, and she draws from him simple and selfless behaviour and feeling, which are just as much part of his personality as rudeness, as in the touching moment of their walk together:

> Charles Tansley felt an extraordinary pride; felt the wind and the cyclamen and the violets for he was walking with a beautiful woman for the first time in his life. He had hold of her bag.

Even Lily, who likes him least, recognizes that he says things like 'Women can't write, women can't paint' not because he believes them but because they are 'for some reason helpful to him'.

His feelings and Lily's appreciation of them are displayed with irony and subtlety in Section 17 of *The Window*, while they are having dinner. Tansley desperately wants to make an impression on the conversation but lacks the *savoir-faire* to make his own opening and sits despising the superficial chat of Mrs. Ramsay and Bankes. Lily understands his feelings and tries an experiment, typical of her own detached attitude to people; she expresses her antagonism to him by a teasing invitation to accompany her to the lighthouse and this produces a rude and childish reaction from Tansley, expressive of his sensitivity to criticism. Lily has to abandon this truth game, however, because Mrs. Ramsay, who is nervous but wants things to go smoothly, silently implores Lily's help in making the party comfortable, and so, in nearly the same words, but with a change of feeling, she again asks him to take her to the lighthouse. He takes the opportunity and begins to blossom forth in talk; now his egoism is satisfied and he is able to shine, for he is intelligent and well informed.

The irony of all this tells us a lot about Tansley, and also about Lily, in whose thoughts the irony mainly exists. Both her invitations to Tansley are lies; the first is recognized by him as a lie and he sees the true feeling of antagonism that produced it and so they understand one another for a moment. But the necessities of polite social relationships produce Lily's second invitation, the insincerity of which Tansley does not realize. Lily feels that their relationship is therefore falsified; the need for politeness has involved her in false behaviour, which has not been seen as false:

> She had done the usual trick—been nice. She would never know him. He would never know her. Human relations were all like that, she thought.

Even in the most intimate and most fully explored relationship in the novel, that of Mr. and Mrs. Ramsay, there is a note of pretence. Mrs. Ramsay is forced to praise him to his face and to bolster up his confidence in a way she feels should not be necessary. His constant need to be reassured, his fear of failure, his resentment that he has achieved less than he should have and that his books will not last, pervert his judgment, leading him to see in praise of other men's works disparagement of himself. This aspect of Ramsay, emphasized by the impartiality of Bankes, puts a strain on his wife and she has to conceal things from him:

> ... to be afraid that he might guess ... that his last book was not quite his best book ... and then to hide small daily things, and the children seeing it, and the burden it laid on them—all this diminished the entire joy. ...

On his side too there is a reserve; her pessimistic conviction of the misery of life distresses him, and he cannot communicate with her in her moods of sadness. But his dependence on her and her respect and reverence for him balance these areas of difference.

The Window traces the pattern of their relationship from one extreme to the other. They are seen at their furthest apart when their disagreement about going to the lighthouse brings out the difference in their attitudes to life:

> 'Damn you,' he said. But what had she said? Simply that it might be fine tomorrow. So it might.
> Not with the barometer falling and the wind due west.

Mr. Ramsay, who believes that children must be taught to face facts and know that life is hard, is infuriated by what seems to him his wife's dishonesty:

> The extraordinary irrationality of her remark, the folly of women's minds enraged him ... she flew in the face of facts, made her children hope what was utterly out of the question, in effect, told lies.

Mrs. Ramsay, who believes in making people happy, in protecting children from losing the contented innocence of childhood, finds her husband's attitude equally repugnant:

> To pursue truth with such astonishing lack of considera-tion of people's feelings, to rend the veils of civilization so wantonly, so brutally was to her . . . an outrage of human decency. . . .

But from this statement of difference they immediately begin to come together again with Ramsay's apology, and the rest of *The Window*, though the idea of their difference recurs, moves towards the moment at the end, when the firm asperity of the masculine mind, which she admires in him, curbs her gloomy thoughts and she is able, though indirectly, to assure him of her love. The fluctuation of feeling between these extremes is conveyed to us in the reflections of the characters and gives us a sense of a growing understanding of their relationship and of them. The source of our understanding is, I would suggest, Virginia Woolf's skill in what can only be called characterization.

Though I understand why Virginia Woolf's methods of presenting character have led critics to call her characters vague, indefinite, unconvincing, unmemorable, I cannot sympathize with such attitudes, which seem to imply that there are standard qualities for fictional characters and that novelists are continually trying to equal or outdo writers of the past. The critics who want hard-edged, definite, neatly summed-up characters, as much as those who want a 'good story', are simply expressing a latent wish that Virginia Woolf should have written books closer to some imagined 'normal' novel. What matters is surely to value what Virginia Woolf could offer which another novelist could not, what her own individual outlook and talent enabled her to create. The main characters of *To the Lighthouse* may be composed of fluctuating feeling, may seem inconsistent and may be used by the novelist to illustrate her general ideas, but the cumulative effect on the reader of 'living in the minds of her characters' is a sense of their distinctness of personality. The characters of Mrs. Ramsay, Mr. Ramsay and Lily Briscoe *are*, to my mind, 'remembered afterwards on their own account', but remembered in a way particular to their author.

If one does try to describe or analyse the characters simply, it is very easy to make them sound like cardboard figures designed to fit into a symbolic pattern, or as mouthpieces for Virginia Woolf's own notions about life. To those who know her other novels, Mrs. Ramsay, for instance, inevitably seems a development of Mrs. Ambrose in *The Voyage Out*, and has similarities to characters elsewhere who can create harmony between people and break down their isolation. She is a woman who by the exercise of love for people in general, endeavours to make life happy and comfortable for them; for the poor by her exercise of philanthropy, for her children by fostering their talents, for her husband by sympathy and reassurance; by encouraging people to marry or to get on well together she creates communication between them. Because her own view of life tends to pessimism she is moved to make every endeavour to create what order she can from the chaos of life.

This is the kind of general description we are bound to make if we try to analyse her or to show the moral basis of her character. Criticism tends to generalize and to classify, but, when we are reading the book we find that the bare bones have a lot more flesh on them than the description suggests, and than is recognized by those who, like George Sampson, have criticized Virginia Woolf's characters as 'the transient and embarrassed phantoms of her ideas'. Though ideas about life, time, art and so on are important themes in her books, it was from an interest in people that she developed them, and we distort the novel if we see it as metaphysics in fiction, just as we distort the characters if we give them a definition which the author denied they possessed. We must try to remain true to the impressions we receive as we read; there we see in Mrs. Ramsay rather than a bringer of peace, a woman who laughs with joy at the thought of marrying a man with a gold watch in a watch-leather bag, who likes circuses and poetry, who pities bachelors, who worries about bulbs but not clothes and so on. Her personality has to be found among all these separate pieces and, if we do try to analyse it and give it a shape, we have to remember that the shape is like the pattern in a kaleidoscope, which will shift and seem different each time we look.

The great richness of detail in the presentation of the main characters, a richness which prevents our having a simple unmixed reaction to them, is produced largely by the novel's 'multiple point of view'—a phrase which I had better explain. The point of view of a novel comes from the way the author chooses to show us his characters and their world. We see the action of *Jane Eyre*, for example, from the point of view of the main character, in whose personality the novelist has sunk her own; in *Wuthering Heights* the view is that of two contrasting narrators who are both bystanders not fully involved in the emotional turmoil of the main characters; in *Pride and Prejudice* the author directs the action as an impersonal voice, which speaks to us in a tone of cool and amused irony, whereas in

Vanity Fair we are addressed openly by the author telling us how to regard the action and speaking of the characters as puppets. I could obviously multiply examples but these few will show some of the ways in which an author can direct our response to his fiction; we are, in any novel, being shown people and actions from a particular angle; we may be given a one-sided or many-sided account; we may be emotionally involved or detached.

To the Lighthouse has a multiple point of view in that, while parts of the novel are narrated in an impersonal author's voice, much of it comes to us from the point of view of the characters. These characters are both observed and observers (though some observe more than others) and so their natures and their relationships are complex and full of irony.

Irony is most operative in the presentation of Mr. Ramsay, who is seen much more from outside than his wife, since we are given only a few passages which present his feelings and thoughts directly. One view we have of him is comic. He is seen as a great blundering buffoon, stalking round the garden, booming poetry at the hedges. His bad temper, self-pity and self-dramatization and the disparity between what he says about facing up to the hardness of life and his own petty resentment of the least of its difficulties, all expose him to ridicule. This aspect of him is epitomized in the comic encounter with Lily early in Part III, where Virginia Woolf creates a superb picture of melodramatic dejection on one side:

> . . . he had assumed a pose of extreme decrepitude; he even tottered a little as he stood there

and spinsterish fastidiousness on the other:

> His immense self-pity . . . spread itself in pools at her

feet and all she did . . . was to draw her skirts a little
closer round her ankles, lest she should get wet.

Lily's accidental success in solacing his soul by praising
his boots sets the ironic seal on this comedy of manners.

But against this picture of a comic self-deceiver, in the
tradition of Parson Adams, we have to set Lily's respect
for his work and his total lack of worldliness, Mrs.
Ramsay's love and reverence for him, his simple unaffected
response to the humanity of Scott's novels and the hard-
ships of the fisherman's life, his genuine courage. The last
view we have of him, through the eyes of his children,
in a moment of achievement and selflessness, seems far
from the tottering actor:

> He rose and stood in the bow of the boat, very straight
> and tall, for all the world, James thought, as if he were
> saying: 'There is no God', and Cam thought, as if he
> were leaping into space, and they both rose to follow him
> as he sprang, lightly like a young man, holding his
> parcel, on to the rock.

It is a tribute to Virginia Woolf's handling of the multiple
point of view that such extremes of character do not seem
arbitrarily yoked together but can be shown working
together, as they are in Section 6 of *The Window*. Here,
Mr. Ramsay's quest for truth is associated by imagery
with deeds of heroic endeavour and exploration, which
both provide a fantastic picture of him marching through
the alphabet equipped with six biscuits and a flask of
water and suggest his masculine strength of mind, his
true courage and his exaggerated sense of courage, his
simplicity and his self-delusion. It is the impersonal
voice of the author which brings out the irony here:

> ... who shall blame the leader of the doomed expedition, if, having adventured to the uttermost, and used his strength wholly to the last ounce and fallen asleep not much caring if he wakes or not, he now perceives by some pricking in his toes that he lives, and does not on the whole object to live, but requires sympathy and whisky. ...

The use of anticlimax is typical of the author's combination of detachment and involvement. We are continually faced with the deflation of a character's self-esteem, or the pricking of a bubble of rhetoric; the fine aspirations of the artist exist in Lily beside the knowledge that her painting will probably be bad, and even Mrs. Ramsay is led, by Carmichael's lack of response to her, to suspect her own motives and to see that she might be accused of wanting power over people and that her philanthropy might seem designed to win praise.

Virginia Woolf said of the true self in an essay:

> We are streaked, variegated, all of a mixture, the colours have run.

By the use of the multiple point of view, and of a flexible prose style which can be, among other things, matter of fact, ironic, lyrical, intense or relaxed, Virginia Woolf conveyed this sense of variegation and created a picture of her characters with such richness and complexity of texture that such questions as 'What does it all mean?', 'How does one judge people?' and so on do not seem empty or rhetorical. She has dramatized the complexity which justifies the questions.

If the reader feels, after reading *The Window* and *Time Passes*, conscious only of the complexity and richness and not of a clear understanding of what to make of the multiplicity of view, that is as it should be; he is in the position of Lily at the beginning of *The Lighthouse*. Hers is the main observing eye in the rest of the book and as she tries to create a painting, she tries to come to terms with the past, dipping into experience as she dips into paint. Mrs. Ramsay is now part of the past and Mr. Ramsay moves away from her towards the lighthouse; their distance from her enables Lily to see more clearly, and though she recognizes that one's vision must constantly be renewed, shows us how in symbol and through the power of art we can reach a kind of understanding.

Questions

1. What do we learn about the character of Lily Briscoe through the eyes of (*a*) William Bankes, (*b*) Mrs. Ramsay, (*c*) herself?

2. Discuss Virginia Woolf's presentation of minor characters by examining (*a*) the Ramsay children, (*b*) Paul Rayley, (*c*) Mrs. McNab.

3. Analyse the development in the character of James.

4. What is the function in the novel of the characters of Augustus Carmichael and Minta Doyle?

5. What aspects of human relationships are shown by the friendships of (*a*) Lily and Bankes, (*b*) Ramsay and Bankes, (*c*) Bankes and Mrs. Ramsay?

6. What examples of failure of communication between one character and another can you find in the novel? What aspects of the characters do they show?

7. Consider the differences in the attitudes of Mr. and Mrs. Ramsay to their children.

IV. IMAGERY AND SYMBOLISM

General

The English language is crammed with figurative expressions (I've just used one), and few writers choose to avoid them, since figurative language is a basic way of giving colour, complexity and richness of association to verse and prose. Such language is particularly necessary to an author who is trying to convey sense-impressions, for sights, sounds, smells, and so on are difficult to render in words without some comparison of one sensation with another. Because Virginia Woolf was trying to describe intense experience and to create for the reader the impressions made upon her characters by what they see and do, her prose is particularly rich in imagery. By its means the novel's range of reference is also extended; some novels have richness of action or of scene, this one richness of detail; though the immediate subject is limited the sense of life is not, since the minds of the characters can range over the whole world.

To the Lighthouse has many pictorial images, such as Mr. Carmichael 'basking with his yellow cat's eyes ajar', or the sea 'stretched like silk across the bay', which make their point clearly and need no individual comment. They are what one might call 'simple' images, similes and metaphors which add a touch of vividness and help the reader to enter the created world.

The more complex images in the novel have greater importance, and awareness and understanding of them greatly add to one's sense of the book's richness and its themes. I cannot hope to discuss all the types of imagery in

To the Lighthouse but have selected several which seem to me significant; these are groups of images, recurrent images, symbolism or association of idea and object, and personification. I shall discuss the symbolism of poetry and literature and of the lighthouse in separate sections.

The most obvious grouped images are those associated with Mr. Ramsay. Such descriptions of him as 'lean as a knife', 'fierce as a hawk', 'like a lion seeking whom he could devour', though they occur in quite different parts of the book, obviously belong together. They can be seen as the smallest threads in a strand of masculine or 'heroic' imagery, which Virginia Woolf uses to convey Mr. Ramsay's nature, his effect on others, and Mrs. Ramsay's respect for the masculine world of actions and things. In his philosophical questioning he is compared to an explorer leading a 'desolate expedition across the icy solitudes of the Polar region', a leader who 'knows that he must lay himself down and die before morning comes'; he stands 'like a desolate sea-bird, alone'. These images, as I have mentioned, have a note of irony but convey the loneliness of Mr. Ramsay's mental life and his stern attitude and, moreover, give him an aura of grandeur. Though we see that he can be petty, vain and tyrannical, the power of association in such images and in the verse he recites helps to convince the reader of his essential fineness. In Part II the lonely questioner of life, pacing the shore at night, inevitably recalls Mr. Ramsay in his solitary walks and in Part III his journey to the lighthouse with James and Cam is seen in terms of the old image of the leader:

> He had all the appearance of a leader making ready for an expedition. . . . They looked . . . as if fate had devoted them to some stern enterprise. . . .

The effect of such images is cumulative; they help to convey an aspect of Ramsay and also give significance to the journey itself. By his presence the voyage becomes an expedition or an enterprise—something which Cam and James both recognize in their different ways. The reaching of the lighthouse is not just the end of a sea-side trip; it is made to seem an achievement.

Virginia Woolf used similar associated images in her description of Mrs. Ramsay. She has been described early in the book as having the courtesy of a 'queen raising from the mud a beggar's dirty foot' and later descends the stairs 'like some queen, who, finding her people gathered in the hall, looks down upon them, and descends among them, and acknowledges their tributes silently'. She is coupled in passing references with Queen Victoria and Helen of Troy, and Lily sees her as a storehouse of wisdom like the 'tombs of kings' containing treasures. On the other hand her directness and simplicity are conveyed by comparisons to a stone, a bird and an arrow; she stands 'still like a tree which has been tossing and quivering and now, when the breeze falls, settles, leaf by leaf, into quiet'. After satisfying her husband's demand for sympathy she seemed 'to fold herself together, one petal closed in another'. This combination of the regal and exotic with natural images of tree and flower helps to create a sense of the fascination of Mrs. Ramsay—the mixture of simple goodness and sophisticated aloofness and beauty which make her the centre of the book.

It is natural that groups of images should form around the characters in a novel, since the novelist wishes to show consistent threads of behaviour. The second type of complex image which I want to distinguish, the recurrent image, is related more to the ideas and themes of the book. One of these themes is the nature of love, the different forms it can take and the way it affects people differently. Mr. and Mrs. Ramsay love one another but her way of loving is distinct from his, as we see from many incidents and thoughts in *The Window*. The most outright expression of the difference is found in a figurative passage in Section 7, when Mr. Ramsay comes to his wife begging sympathy; Mrs. Ramsay's response and his dependence on her are described as follows:

> Mrs. Ramsay . . . seemed to raise herself with an effort, and at once to pour erect into the air a rain of energy, a column of spray . . . and into this delicious fecundity, this fountain and spray of life, the fatal sterility of the male plunged itself, like a beak of brass, barren and bare. . . .'

and again:

> . . . James felt all her strength flaring up to be drunk and quenched by the beak of brass, the arid scimitar of the male, which smote mercilessly, again and again, demanding sympathy.

This violent and unusual image, with its strong sexual element, conveys very forcibly the relationship of the two and their different ways of love, his aggressive and demanding, hers sweet and generous. The difference between them is apparent to the child James and when, in Part III with James now fifteen, Virginia Woolf presents his thoughts about his father, she returns to the earlier image —linking it to James's own violent symbol of his Oedipal relationship with Mr. Ramsay, 'striking his father to the heart'—

Only now, as he grew older . . . it was not him . . .
whom he wanted to kill, but it was the thing that
descended on him . . . that fierce sudden black-
winged harpy, with its talons and its beak all cold and
hard, that struck and struck at you.

This train of thought echoes the childhood scene and he
remembers his feelings:

something flourished up in the air, something arid and
sharp descended even there, like a blade, a scimitar,
smiting through the leaves and flowers even of that
happy world and making them shrivel and fall.

The conflict of feeling in James about his father, whom
he hates and fears while longing for his approval, is not
completely resolved at the end of the book, but in this
figurative passage (which I have only selected brief
extracts from) Virginia Woolf is showing James working
out his feelings and beginning to come to terms with the
confusions inherent in human relationships. By using a
recurring image she shows how feelings in the present
develop from past experience. The beak of brass and the
scimitar represent an aspect of love which is true to life,
but the novelist's skill and subtlety lie in the way she has
carried on the image to express something of the complexity of family relationships.

The nature of love is illuminated by another violent and
repeated image, which occurs to Lily at the dinner table
when she feels first attracted by Paul's love for Minta, and
then repelled by his indifference to everyone else.

He turned on her cheek the heat of love, its horror, its
cruelty, its unscrupulosity. It scorched her and Lily,

looking at Minta . . . flinched for her exposed to those fangs and was thankful. For at any rate . . . she need not marry.

When in Part III Lily considers this love, with the ironical knowledge that the marriage had not turned out well, the image recurs but the fire itself now has the double aspect of irony:

> the roar and crackle repelled her with fear and disgust, as if while she saw its splendour and power she saw too how it fed on the treasure of the house, greedily, disgustingly and she loathed it. But for a sight, for a glory it surpassed everything . . . and burnt like a signal fire on a desert island.

Such recurrences (and there are a number of others) are part of the careful unity of *To the Lighthouse*; they knit the parts together not only by development of the ideas and characters but also by giving a continuity of feeling between past and present. When we recall a feeling we tend to do so by remembering the occasion when we first had it, or remembering some object with which it is connected. Such association of an occasion or object with an idea is a simple kind of symbolism; the object by association comes to stand for the feeling. Thus the fire, which on its first appearance was a metaphor devised to convey Lily's reaction to Paul, has become for her in the later reference a symbol of love. Virginia Woolf used a lot of symbolism of this kind in the novel and it is not difficult to see why she so frequently related ideas and feelings to particular objects. She had chosen as a novelist to concentrate on the inner feelings of her characters and

E

to try to create their sense of life. Because she wanted to present a true picture of life and to deal with 'an ordinary mind on an ordinary day', the action of her novels is deliberately sparse and common-place; the richness and excitement are to be found in the individual reaction of her characters, in their response to ordinary experience and the meaning of their own lives. Thus she moves from outside into her characters' minds, from the object, that is, to the feeling.

In Section 4 of *The Window* she shows William Bankes staring at the sand-dunes and being led to think of his former friendship with Ramsay, and Lily Briscoe thinking of the characters of both men as she stands looking at a tree:

> Standing now, apparently transfixed, by the pear-tree, impressions poured in upon her of those two men, and to follow her thought was like following a voice which speaks too quickly to be taken down by one's pencil, and the voice was her own voice saying without prompting undeniable, everlasting, contradictory things, so that even the fissures and humps on the bark of the pear-tree were irrevocably fixed there for eternity.

She thinks of Ramsay's pettiness, Bankes's greatness, and Ramsay's unworldliness:

> All of this danced up and down, like a company of gnats, each separate, but all marvellously controlled in an invisible elastic net—danced up and down in Lily's mind, in and about the branches of the pear-tree, where still hung in effigy the scrubbed kitchen table, symbol of her profound respect for Mr. Ramsay's mind, until her thought which had spun quicker and quicker exploded

of its own intensity; she felt released; a shot went off close at hand, and there came, flying down from its fragments, frightened, effusive, tumultuous, a flock of starlings.

In this passage Virginia Woolf leads from the garden into Lily's thoughts quite naturally and weaves together the literal and the figurative with beautiful control, so that the images (thoughts like gnats, thoughts exploding) fit the scene—the pear-tree and the shot from Jasper's gun. The characters' thoughts begin from the physical objects and return to them; this relationship of objects and thought forms the characteristic rhythm of the narrative in Part I. The interior monologue could very easily float off into a series of vague feelings and Virginia Woolf prevents this by embedding thought in the sights and sounds of the particular place she has used as setting.

The association of object and feeling, as I have mentioned, very easily becomes symbolism, as in the extract above, the kitchen table comes to stand for Mr. Ramsay's thinking. Similarly the hedge and geraniums at which Ramsay stares, as he paces the garden, represent stages in his logical arguments; the bœuf-en-daube which Mrs. Ramsay serves at dinner becomes a symbol of her pleasure at Paul and Minta's engagement and at Bankes's presence; James's hand on the tiller becomes for Cam symbolic of his firmness of purpose, and so on. The most interesting of these symbols are, of course, those that occur several times in the book and develop their meaning as the book proceeds. One of these is the lighthouse itself which I shall deal with at greater length in a later section. Another is the pattern in the table-cloth which Lily connects with her painting while at dinner:

She took up the salt-cellar and put it down again on a flower in the pattern in the table-cloth, so as to remind herself to move the tree.

At first merely a reminder, the flower takes on more significance for Lily when she feels again the antagonism of Tansley:

There's the sprig on the table-cloth; there's my painting; I must move the tree to the middle; that matters—nothing else.

This resolution cheers her and sustains her when she feels excluded from the love of Paul. Her painting is her independence and when she visits the house again, years later, she remembers her moment of revelation and the symbol connected with it. It had protected her from marriage, like a talisman:

She had only escaped by the skin of her teeth though, she thought. She had been looking at the table-cloth, and it had flashed upon her that she would move the tree to the middle, and need never marry anybody, and she had felt an enormous exultation.

So the spray develops from a reminder, to a defence against men like Tansley, a protection from the passion of love, an inspiration, and eventually even a sign of her triumph over Mrs. Ramsay, who planned the marriage of Paul and Minta and was trying to manœuvre Lily into marriage with Bankes. Her feminism, her individuality, her integrity have been preserved and the symbol of her preservation is carried in her mind.

Virginia Woolf's concentration in Parts I and III on the individual characters' reactions and attempts to see a meaning in life led her to use symbolism as her main type of imagery in these sections and I hope I have shown why the use of symbol is appropriate to her aim. The contrasting attitude of *Time Passes*, with its subordination of individual human characters to the forces of time and nature, is clearly marked by Virginia Woolf's turning to other types of image and figurative expression. Symbols do occur (the lighthouse and the empty house, for example) and the section includes many examples of simple images, since it is deliberately pictorial as well as abstract; simile, for instance, is used to describe Mrs. McNab, who 'rolled like a ship at sea', and who, moving through the sunlit rooms, 'looked like a tropical fish oaring its way through sun-lanced waters'. But more striking here is the use of the elevated or rhetorical figures of speech, such as personification and the extended simile.

Personification is particularly frequent; very near the beginning of Part II the approaching darkness has turned into something like an animal:

> darkness . . . creeping in at keyholes and crevices, stole round window blinds, came into bedrooms, swallowed up here a jug and basin, there a bowl of red and yellow dahlias. . . .

Later we find the same device applied to the air, the wind, night, nature, spring, loveliness and so on. The use of this figure of speech reflects the shift in perspective of which I have already spoken; the abstract forces have here become the actors and human beings are reduced to their playthings and so abstractions take on the active role in the language. They have their own power and act as individuals, as when 'the wind sent its spies about the house'. The forces of nature seem indifferent to man:

Did Nature supplement what man advanced? Did she complete what he began? With equal complacence she saw his misery, condoned his meanness and acquiesced in his torture.

yet they have something to say to him if he cares to hear:

Through the open window the voice of the beauty of the world came murmuring . . . entreating the sleepers . . . at least to lift the blind and look out. They would see then night flowing down in purple; his head crowned; his sceptre jewelled; and how in his eyes a child might look.

Personification makes clear that though natural forces may be turned to advantage by men they are independent; men are mortal and nature will outlast them.

The extended comparisons are not frequent but they are also notably rhetorical figures of speech, associated more frequently with poetry than prose. One of them presents the idea of the transience of man in a way designed, in fact, to arouse poetic associations in the reader's mind:

The autumn trees, ravaged as they are, take on the flash of tattered flags kindling in the gloom of cool cathedral caves where gold letters on marble pages describe death in battle and how bones bleach and burn far away in Indian sands.

In the other main example (Part II, Section 7) personification and simile are combined as the chaos of wind and waves is compared to the play of brutal and brainless Leviathans.

Such high rhetoric is necessary to Virginia Woolf's attempt to create the impression she wanted in this 'most difficult abstract piece of writing' in which, as she re-marked in her diary, 'I have to give an empty house, no people's characters, the passage of time, all eyeless and featureless with nothing to cling to'. But she was careful to break up the effect of the abstractions by continual reference back to the house, the remnants of the people who had lived there and the activities of Mrs. McNab and Mrs. Bast. The use of anticlimax which I have mentioned earlier was a defence against the reader's possible objec-tions to finding such elevated style in a piece of prose fiction. The quick switch from one tone to another is well illustrated in the following example:

> Meanwhile the mystic, the visionary, walked on the beach, stirred a puddle, looked at a star and asked themselves: 'what am I? . . .' and suddenly an answer was vouchsafed them . . . so that they were warm in the frost and had comfort in the desert. But Mrs. McNab continued to drink and gossip as before.

Poetry and Literature

Virginia Woolf was an extremely well-read person and could be described, without criticism, as bookish; she not only wrote books, read and reviewed many of the past and present but was also concerned with the actual making of books after she and her husband founded the Hogarth Press in 1917. It is natural that she should use literary references and quotations in her novels, since they are part of her way of life and her way of thinking. There are in *To the Lighthouse* a number of such references, which do not merely suggest the social class of her characters and their attitudes of mind but are used as a deliberate device by means of which ideas can be concisely and suggestively presented.

Some of the quotations are used very simply, but even the snatch of a sea-shanty, 'Damn your eyes, damn your eyes', sung by Minta, shows what an economical device quotation can be. It is a clear expression of Minta's impulsiveness and her excitement on this particular day, and also, in the sense of the words, of her lack of consideration both of the consequences of her actions and of the feelings of Andrew and Nancy, who are forced to sit singing on the cliff when they really want to be exploring rock-pools. Love is shown as arrogant towards those excluded from the magic circle, making them feel awkward and embarrassed, as Andrew and Nancy are when they see Paul and Minta in one another's arms, or frightened and diminished as Lily is at the dinner table when talking to Paul:

> But it was not his meaning—it was the odd chuckle he gave, as if he had said, Throw yourself over the cliff if you like, I don't care.

This particular thread of meaning, the unsympathetic side of love, develops from and is defined by the brief chorus of a song.

Literary references are used we may say to define emotions and relationships in an economical way; they are in fact a kind of symbolism, since they act as signs of more complex ideas than the words of the quotation themselves indicate. Virginia Woolf was concerning herself in *To the Lighthouse* with intense feeling such as is often associated with poetry; quotation from the poetry of others is a way of bringing into her prose something of the feeling of verse and of giving her ideas about the relationship of art to reality a basis in the experience of her characters.

The most important of the literary references are those associated with Mr. and Mrs. Ramsay. One of the characteristics of Mr. Ramsay which is repeatedly referred to is his habit of reciting verse aloud. This was a habit of Sir Leslie Stephen and she had already used it in her first novel, *The Voyage Out*, as a characteristic of Mr. Ambrose, another figure based upon her father. But, whereas in the early book it had appeared merely a comic eccentricity, in *To the Lighthouse* the idea is used more seriously and the quotations seem deliberately selected for their associations. The comedy is still there, as when Mrs. Ramsay remembers her husband's bursting out 'Best and brightest come away!' to a startled spinster. But more serious aspects of Mr. Ramsay's character are also brought out by means of these explosions. They are expressions of his emotional nature for, though he is intellectual and spends much of his time in abstract thought, his emotions are near to the surface, readily aroused and unrestrainedly expressed. He is, as we have seen, vulnerable to others' ridicule. This is brought out fully in the course of *The Window*, particularly in his wife's thoughts and in the conversation at dinner, but this aspect of Ramsay has already been suggested to the reader in the picture of him stalking up and down the garden, alternately muttering and declaiming Tennyson's *Charge of the Light Brigade*. 'Someone had blundered' is used to link together several ideas: Ramsay's own blunder in making an exhibition of himself, his literal blundering into Lily and Bankes, their reactions to it and the quick protective instinct of his wife who realizes that he may appear foolish. In the third part of the book this same habit defines his feelings and the reactions of others to him, when his tendency to dramatize himself and to make a public display of his grief at his wife's death is represented in the repeated use of the lines from Cowper:

> We perished each alone,
> But I beneath a rougher sea
> And whelmed in deeper gulfs than he.

These words cause great embarrassment to Cam and James when he groans them aloud in the boat but, though his emotion is exaggerated, the lines are not inappropriate to his situation, since they develop the idea of the isolation of the individual which other parts of the book support.

It is significant that both these poems are examples of what one might call manly or heroic verse: the Tennyson poem about military heroism and Cowper's *The Castaway* telling an anecdote of a man lost at sea, who died bravely during one of Anson's voyages. These examples of courage can obviously be connected with the imagery associated with Ramsay.

The literary images connected with Mrs. Ramsay also suggest her nature to the reader and define her own feelings and the reactions of other characters to her. She is occupied for much of the time in *The Window* in reading to James and the Grimms' fairy tale she is reading becomes one of the threads connecting together the various parts of the narrative as a reference to it turns our attention from the thoughts of Lily or Ramsay to the mother and child at the window.

At dinner the lines quoted from *Luriana Lurilee* lodge in her mind and lead her later in the evening to pick up a book of poetry; the lines also give to the end of the dinner a heightened significance and move Carmichael to express his respect for Mrs. Ramsay. He is the one character who appears to stand aloof from her but here he pays her homage by addressing the poetry directly to her. It is clear that Virginia Woolf means us to understand that to the artist one must speak in a special way; only when the spirit and quality of Mrs. Ramsay are expressed in formal, even symbolic terms can the poet appreciate her; he responds to the idea of her rather than directly to her conversation or personality.

This idea of a poem as a symbol of a person's qualities connects closely with the most 'literary' part of the book, the scene between Mr. and Mrs. Ramsay at the end of *The Window*. As Mr. Ramsay, led to take up a novel by Scott by the conversation at dinner, responds emotionally to the pathos, humour and sanity of Scott's story, so, also remembering the earlier conversation, Mrs. Ramsay reads a book of poems. At first she reads randomly, seeking refreshment in the beauty of poetic images and letting her mind float vaguely. Virginia Woolf represents this by the opening lines of William Browne's *The Siren's Song*:

Steer, hither steer your winged pines,
                                        all beaten mariners.

That this, like the shanty and *The Castaway*, is a sea poem is not accidental; Virginia Woolf remarked in her diary 'the sea is to be heard all through it'. Mrs. Ramsay's search for direction and help in the poems is suggested in the sense of the line and the fact that this is expressed in an image of the sea connects with the symbol of the lighthouse. The poem to which Mrs. Ramsay is steered is Shakespeare's sonnet: 'I have been absent from you in the spring' and through her experience of reading this, feeling cleansed, rested and satisfied, she moves towards her husband, repeating the final line: 'As with your shadow I with these did play.' Though the shadows of her pessimism and his desire for encouragement once again lie behind their conversation, they are now able to help one another, he to curb her fears, she to reassure him of her love. The implication is that through their reading and response to what they have read they have become more responsive to one another; their emotions have been drawn out of themselves towards the other. So the power to communicate is augmented by the moving power of art.

The Lighthouse

The reader of *To the Lighthouse* is prepared to find the idea of the journey to the lighthouse of importance in the book before he even begins to read it, since titles of novels do usually point to a central figure or idea. Other novels by Virginia Woolf, *The Voyage Out* and *Between the Acts*, for example, show two similar uses of a title with both a literal and a figurative meaning which becomes apparent in the course of the book. When we do open the covers of the novel and read, we find that it begins and ends with the lighthouse and that the framework of the narrative is the undertaking and eventual achievement of a visit to it. References to the journey recur throughout Part I, the lighthouse is mentioned in Part II, and Part III is almost entirely occupied by the journey to it. So the idea is present in our minds for almost the whole book. This recurrence means that we are continually being made conscious of the characters' feelings about the journey and the significance the lighthouse has for them. It is another example of an object becoming so closely associated with feelings and ideas that it comes to have symbolic force in the book.

It is with reference to the lighthouse, indeed, that the association of personal feeling and an object is most clearly stated, when Mrs. Ramsay, sitting alone after James has been sent to bed, looks out and sees the beam of light, two short strokes and one long steady beam:

> . . . which was her stroke, for watching them in this mood always at this hour one could not help attaching oneself to one thing especially of the things one saw. . . . Often she found herself sitting and looking, sitting and looking, with her work in her hands until she became the thing she looked at—that light for example.

But though Mrs. Ramsay identifies herself with the beam she does not associate one particular emotion with it; it seems ambiguous. It is impersonal, 'the steady light, the pitiless, the remorseless', and yet its light on the water brings a moment of great beauty:

> the ecstasy burst in her eyes and waves of pure delight raced over the floor of her mind and she felt, It is enough! It is enough!

The ambiguity here is characteristic, for elsewhere we find the lighthouse associated with conflicting emotions. Its first appearance is as the subject of the opening conversation in the novel, a conversation which brings out differences of opinion between Mr. and Mrs. Ramsay and which culminates in Mr. Ramsay's outburst of anger, which I have already quoted. It is from this conversation that the lighthouse takes on its symbolic force, since it has been used as the object which defines two opposing attitudes to life; it is as a consequence in terms of the lighthouse expedition that Mr. and Mrs. Ramsay make up their quarrel, when he offers to ask the coastguard about the weather (thus deferring to her views) and she, at the end of Part I, expresses her love by conceding that he was right:

> Yes, you were right. It's going to be wet tomorrow. She had not said it (*i.e. that she loved him*) but he knew it. And she looked at him smiling. For she had triumphed again.

The lighthouse appears from such use as a goal towards which different characters have different reactions. This object outside the characters themselves can, by the accumulated references to it, very easily be seen as symbolizing the idea of aim itself and of the attitudes to it which the characters express. But the opposition of attitudes makes it a symbol of difference as well. The nature of a lighthouse can readily be expressed in terms of opposites: it is a piece of land in the sea, a point of stillness in the moving water, a light in the dark, security in danger. It can be seen as a sign of man's control over nature, since he put it there to protect his fellow men, but it can also be seen, isolated by the sea, as an impersonal, detached thing sending its constant light to probe the land like some supernatural observer. Some of these aspects are used in *To the Lighthouse*. The light is seen as indifferent to man by Mrs. Ramsay and also in the references to it in *Time Passes*, but it is also a place where men live without companionship or newspapers, the object of a pious pilgrimage in memory of Mrs. Ramsay and part of Cam's romantic daydream about shipwreck at sea.

Virginia Woolf comes to terms with this diversity most clearly in her development of the feelings of James. As a

child his passionate desire to go to the lighthouse had
been thwarted, as he thinks, by his father; as a young man
he goes to the lighthouse in his father's company but
unwillingly, because again he has been coerced. As they
near the lighthouse itself James remembers the childhood
scene, his mother and father's disagreement and his own
feelings:

> The Lighthouse was then a silvery, misty-looking
> tower with a yellow eye that opened suddenly and
> softly in the evening. Now—
> James looked at the Lighthouse. He could see the
> white-washed rocks; the tower, stark and straight; he
> could see that it was barred with black and white. . . . So
> that was the Lighthouse, was it?
> No, the other was also the Lighthouse. For nothing
> was simply one thing.

The association of the 'misty-looking tower' with his
mother is clear from the context here, and that 'the
tower stark and straight' is associated with his father is
made clear in Section 13:

> So it was like that, James thought, the Lighthouse . . .
> a stark tower on a bare rock. It satisfied him. It con-
> firmed some feeling of his own about his own character.
> . . . He looked at his father. . . . They shared that
> knowledge. 'We are driving before a gale—we must
> sink,' he began saying to himself, half aloud exactly as
> his father said it.

James thus moves towards his father, overcomes his
resentment and resolves his own conflict, for the moment,
through the symbolic journey; the lighthouse still has

more than one meaning but the meanings can exist
together.

If we have to state what the lighthouse stands for, we
must allow for this ambivalence and associate it with the
ambiguity of life itself, an ambiguity which *To the
Lighthouse* presents in many ways and in all three main
characters. The three attitudes to life which they embody
are all partly revealed by the symbol. Mrs. Ramsay
reaches out to the lighthouse, though it is pitiless, by a
sense of identification and joy. Mr. Ramsay achieves the
journey to a 'bare bleak reality' with his sandwiches and
his parcel, having cast off, if only for the moment, his
limitations of sympathy and concern with himself. Lily
reaches it by proxy, by her understanding and the
imaginative sympathy with which she enters the experience
of others. These relationships to the symbol can all be
seen as images of their lives. But Virginia Woolf kept the
idea of ambiguity in the reader's mind to the end. It is
most clearly summed up in the voice of Lily, the observer,
in terms of painting:

> One wanted, she thought, dipping her brush de-
> liberately, to be on a level with ordinary experience, to
> feel simply that's a chair, that's a table, and yet at the
> same time, It's a miracle, it's an ecstasy.

Questions

1. I have had space only to mention what I have called
'simple' imagery in the novel, but there is quite a lot
that could be said about it. You might examine, among
the many types of image, the use and effect of (*a*) images of
water, (*b*) images of colour, (*c*) sound images, (*d*) flowers.

2. Examine the images associated with Mrs. Ramsay and show their combined effect.

3. Consider the passages concerning Lily's picture and discuss the ideas connected with it.

4. Analyse the diverse means by which Virginia Woolf suggested the constant presence of the sea.

5. I have mentioned Virginia Woolf's use of the story Mrs. Ramsay is reading to James as a connecting thread. What other purposes does it serve?

6. Read Cowper's *The Castaway* and Shakespeare's sonnet 'I have been absent from you in the spring', and then comment on Virginia Woolf's use of the two poems.

7. I have said very little about the character of Cam, though she is one of the more important figures in the later part of the book. What aspects of her would you say are shown: (*a*) through literary references and quotations? (*b*) with reference to the lighthouse and the journey to it?

F

V. ANALYSIS OF PART I, SECTION 17

I have chosen to write about the dinner party because it forms the emotional climax of *The Window*. In the earlier sections we have gradually been shown the nature and relationships of the characters, one by one, and now they are all brought together and we can see the whole community which they form. In this movement from individual encounters to a scene involving the whole group we can see, as in other features of the book, similarities to musical structure; compare, for example, Benjamin Britten's *Young Person's Guide to the Orchestra* where the instruments, first heard separately, join together for the final fugue. The section is typical in its narrative method, with the continual weaving together of conversation and the characters' thoughts. It is not perhaps so typical of the novel in other ways. It is longer than any other individual section and it is much more of a 'set-piece' than any other part; it is the nearest to a dramatic scene with the whole cast assembled and set in motion by the author. But because it is a 'set-piece', with its own beginning, development and end, it is more readily detached from its context than most of the other parts.

As befits a formalized scene, the dinner is heralded at the end of the preceding section; the striking of the gong and the bustle of activity as people gather from the various parts of the house for dinner lead into the scene. It is this sense of formal announcement that makes one regard the scene as a set-piece; the opening sentences of *Time Passes* work in a similar way. The section itself however begins not with description of the scene but by taking us once more into the thoughts of Mrs. Ramsay. The action develops, characteristically, on two planes: the concerns of the present moment, her duties as hostess, struggle with her simultaneous mood of despair. The room, with the table laid and the guests seating themselves, is shown to us through her eyes, seeming at this moment charmless, empty, remote. Even her love for her husband has ebbed away, leaving her indifferent to his frowning face at the other end of the table. Because of her mood the people at the table seem isolated from one another, like detached fragments waiting to be welded together:

> Nothing seemed to have merged. They all sat separate. And the whole of the effort of merging and flowing and creating rested on her.

From this opening, showing us Mrs. Ramsay's gloom and the isolation of human beings in themselves, the action develops to show how her mood changes and to create for us the ebb and flow of feelings in her and others as they react to the conversation and to one another. We see gradually how the 'merging and flowing and creating' are achieved, so that the dinner party becomes a success and isolation is resolved into a mood of happy social inter-course. One way of analysing the section would be to follow this fluctuation of feeling in sequence, to see how skilfully Virginia Woolf develops one thought from another, moves from one character to another and in and out of their minds, but this aspect of the section is obvious to the attentive reader and I will satisfy myself with one example only of her careful harmony of style.

Mrs. Ramsay feels, as we have seen, cut off from what is going on around her and the author uses an image to help express this; it is as if she is drifting apart from a current

of moving water: 'she felt, more and more strongly, outside that eddy'. When, moved by her mistaken pity for
Bankes, she leaves her self-regarding pessimism and begins
to exert her sociable habits and look after the needs of her
guests, this is expressed in a simile which is appropriate
to the former image:

> in pity for him, life being now strong enough to bear
> her on again, she began all this business, as a sailor not
> without weariness sees the wind fill his sail.

The movement from Mrs. Ramsay's thoughts to those of
Lily, who sits watching her, is accomplished smoothly by
continuing the image of the sailing ship, first drifting
aimlessly away and then turning to set its course into the
sun. Imagery thus dovetails one reaction neatly into
another and this is typical of Virginia Woolf's skill in
creating an impression of fluidity and of perfect naturalness
in leaving one subject and taking up another. The sense
of unity achieved in this way is a feature of the whole
novel.

Less obvious than such examples of the novelist's
control over the sequence of thought are those features
which give to the section its total or cumulative effect, the
particular aspects of people that she chooses to display
for instance and the viewpoint of characters and narrator.

Consider the treatment of Mrs. Ramsay. As we read we
see how her mood changes as a result of successive events
(her husband's anger with Carmichael, the arrival of
Paul and Minta, the success of the bœuf-en-daube and
so on), but we do not perhaps notice at first how these
changes of mood add to our experience of Mrs. Ramsay.
Here is one of Virginia Woolf's most evocative creations
of the individual's sense of life, the 'semi-transparent

envelope' of being. In the course of the dinner we are shown her pessimism, her pity for Bankes, her pleasure at having him as a guest, the experience of past friends she has shared with him, her feelings of inadequacy and need for Lily's help, her hope that they will marry, her pleasure at Paul's engagement, her silent conflict with her husband's irritation, her fear that the conversation may distress him, her interest in the proper preparation of vegetables, and a host of other things. These emotions are all natural to the occasion which produces them and develop from one another in a way which is logical and yet full of suggestion of the precariousness of human feeling. The novelist succeeds here in creating that sense of the reality and truth of the life her characters lead which, as I mentioned at the beginning of this book, Virginia Woolf saw as one of the basic aims of all novelists. It is there as much in the relationship of Tansley's egoism and aggressiveness to his private humiliation and in the feelings of Lily, which I discussed in Section III.

The evocation of a scene in which the natures and relationships of her characters are demonstrated is the basic purpose of Section 17, but the richness of their experience and the psychological truth with which this is conveyed, do not in themselves explain why the section strikes the reader as significant and moving. Explanation of this has to take into account the way the scene is shaped and focused for the reader.

There is, for one thing, a strong visual interest in the scene. It is most apparent in the passage describing the bowl of fruit which Rose has arranged and the effect of candlelight on the room and the table and people surrounding it. The result of lighting the candles is to bring the party together, to enclose the guests and to make a unified group from what had been individual personalities. At the moment when Paul and Minta are to join the group, and the great brown dish is to be brought in, a sense of harmony and communion is conveyed by this picture of the faces in the circle of light. This descriptive passage takes up and develops a sense of place which has already been implied. We, the readers, and the narrator seem to be stationed at one end of the table, sharing the thoughts of Mrs. Ramsay, moving sometimes to her nearest neighbours, Bankes, Lily and Tansley, but always hovering at the same end of the room, looking down the table, past the children and Carmichael, across the bowl of fruit to Mr. Ramsay at the other end. This is what I mean by saying that the scene is 'focused' for us; we are given a consistent view which holds together the disparate reactions of the characters. The gathering may seem, for example, stiff and meaningless to Mrs. Ramsay at one point, harmonious and pleasant at another, but its elements remained the same for us and give a solid framework to the section. The picture set before us also contains objects with which the thoughts of the characters may be linked and their changes of mood expressed. The bowl of fruit, with its richness of colour and shape, stimulates Mrs. Ramsay's imagination to picture it as a world in itself, and from this image of unity her mind moves to the feeling of sharing pleasure with Carmichael, who is also gazing at the bowl. The candlelit faces, in this moment of sharing emotion with another, are naturally associated with the sense of union:

> here, inside the room, seemed to be order and dry land; there, outside, a reflection in which things wavered and vanished, waterily.

Some change at once went through them all, as if this had really happened, and they were all conscious of making a party together in a hollow, on an island.

The sense of community and order, which is formed by Mrs. Ramsay with the help of Lily and Bankes, and of good food and of the happiness of the engaged couple, is brought out even more clearly in Mrs. Ramsay's later sense of the significance of the present moment:

she had already felt about something different once before that afternoon: there is a coherence in things, a stability; something, she meant, is immune from change, and shines out . . . in the face of the flowing, the fleeting, the spectral, like a ruby; so that again tonight she had the feeling she had had once today already, of peace, of rest. Of such moments, she thought, the thing is made that remains for ever after. This would remain.

That the moment does seem significant to the reader owes much to the shaping or pattern of the section, which is emphasized in several evocative ways. The subject-matter of Section 17, a dinner, implies naturally both a pattern of arrangement, as meat succeeds soup and is succeeded by fruit, and an atmosphere of formality, since it is an occasion when people's actions are public. The sense of occasion is emphasized by the heralding of the scene, the engagement which makes the dinner a celebration, the rarity of Bankes's appearance at Mrs. Ramsay's table and the special dish which has taken so long to prepare. The presentation of Mrs. Ramsay too gives a sense of ceremony to the scene. Earlier she has been seen in informal moments quietly reading and knitting, walking in the garden and dressing for dinner, but now she is invested with the dignity of the hostess, presiding over her table and providing for her guests. It is partly because of the occasion that people feel inhibited, and that Mrs. Ramsay is conscious of the effort she needs to make to bring her guests into harmony, and it is for the same reason that this effort seems significant and important to us. She moves from dispirited languor to the attempt to fuse the separate elements, and the moment of communication takes from the scene this aspect of specialness and is conveyed to us in an action which has almost a feeling of ritual. This is the moment when all voices are stilled except one, that of her husband, whose authority she had missed earlier, saying a poem which all listen to and which gives expression to the feeling of unity:

> She knew without looking round, that everyone at the table was listening to the voice saying:
> > 'I wonder if it seems to you
> > Luriana, Lurilee'
> with the same sort of relief and pleasure that she had, as if this were, at last, the natural thing to say, this were their own voice speaking.

The phrase 'their own voice' would not have been possible when 'they all sat separate' and marks the feeling of unity clearly.

Mrs. Ramsay has brought this about, created 'this moment of friendship and liking', and it is fitting that the ritualized moment should be turned into a compliment to her, as it is by Carmichael. Her spirit is represented to him in the verse and he applies the lines to her and 'bowed to her as if he did her homage'. The reader will see that this picks up one of the threads of imagery associated else-where with Mrs. Ramsay; she is seen here at her most queenly.

However, Virginia Woolf wishes us to see this moment of significance in both its aspects; its meaning is shown in the scene I have just described, its transitory quality in her final paragraph which leads in to the following section:

> she waited a moment longer in a scene which was vanishing even as she looked, and then . . . it changed . . . it had become, she knew, giving one last look at it over her shoulder, already the past.

As part of the past, however, it can still exist in memory and become part of the continuity of life. On her way upstairs Mrs. Ramsay considers the evening, what it has meant and what it will become in the lives of others:

> They would, she thought, going on again, however long they lived, come back to this night; this moon; this wind; this house: and her too. It flattered her, where she was most susceptible of flattery, to think how, wound about in their hearts, however long they lived she would be woven; and . . . the sofa on the landing (her mother's) . . . the rocking chair (her father's). . . . All that would be revived again in the lives of Paul and Minta.

Further Reading

A. *Works by Virginia Woolf*

The novels of Virginia Woolf, in chronological order, are:

1915 *The Voyage Out*
1919 *Night and Day*
1922 *Jacob's Room*
1925 *Mrs. Dalloway*
1927 *To the Lighthouse*
1928 *Orlando*
1931 *The Waves*
1937 *The Years*
1941 *Between the Acts*

All are published by the Hogarth Press, and six are available in Penguin editions.

Her first novel, *The Voyage Out*, makes an interesting comparison with *To the Lighthouse*, and students would probably do well to read that, *Mrs. Dalloway* and *Between the Acts* before *The Waves*, which is not an easy book to read, though it is arguably her finest and certainly the most original in technique.

The essays to which I have referred may be found in the following collections:

Mr. Bennett and Mrs. Brown (first published separately) in
The Captain's Death-Bed
Modern Fiction in *The Common Reader* (First Series)
Reviews of Dorothy Richardson in *Contemporary Writers*
Phases of Fiction in *Granite and Rainbow*
Evening over Sussex in *The Death of the Moth*

The Hogarth Press has recently issued a collected edition of Virginia Woolf's essays in four volumes.

Extracts from Virginia Woolf's diary were edited by her

husband, Leonard Woolf, after her death and published under the title *A Writer's Diary*.

B. *Biographical and Critical Works*

The most intimate view of Virginia Woolf is to be found in her husband's autobiography; obviously, since it is the story of Leonard Woolf's life, much of it is not concerned with her, but it is an absorbing personal and social history, interesting in itself and providing much information which indirectly helps us to understand his wife. Four volumes have so far been published: *Sowing, Growing, Beginning Again* and *Downhill all the Way*.

Biographical information in a more condensed form, together with many photographs, may be found in *Virginia Woolf*, by Monique Nathan (Evergreen Profile Book No. 34, Grove Press Inc., New York, and Evergreen Books Ltd., London, 1961).

J. K. Johnstone's *The Bloomsbury Group* is a study of the group of literary and intellectual people with whom she shared friendship, and discussion.

The most helpful and stimulating general book of criticism is Joan Bennett's *Virginia Woolf—Her Art as a Novelist* (second edition, 1964, published in paper-back by Cambridge).

Other studies include *Virginia Woolf* by E. M. Forster (Rede Lecture, 1942), *Virginia Woolf* by David Daiches (1945), *Virginia Woolf—A Commentary* by Bernard Blackstone (1949). There are useful chapters on Virginia Woolf in *The Modern Age* (Pelican Guide to English Literature, No. 7, ed. Boris Ford, 1961), and in C. B. Cox's *The Free Spirit* (Oxford, 1963).

APPENDIX

LURIANA LURILEE

Most of the poems from which Virginia Woolf quotes in *To the Lighthouse* and which I have discussed in Chapter IV are fairly well known. But the poem recited by Mr. Ramsay and Carmichael at dinner and later recalled by Mrs. Ramsay, 'Come out and climb the garden-path/Luriana, Lurilee', is little known and difficult to trace. I owe my knowledge of its authorship and origin to Mr. Leonard Woolf, who courteously identified it for me.

It was written by Charles Elton (1839–1900), who was related by marriage to Lytton Strachey, author of *Eminent Victorians* and *Queen Victoria*, and a close friend of Virginia Woolf. The poem was not published (except for the extracts in *To the Lighthouse*) until 1945, when it appeared in an anthology, *Another World Than This*, compiled by Victoria Sackville-West and Harold Nicolson (published by Michael Joseph).

As with the other poems referred to in the novel, reading the whole poem does add to one's understanding of why the particular literary reference was used; I have therefore added here the complete text of Elton's poem.

> Come out and climb the garden path,
>   Luriana, Lurilee.
> The china rose is all abloom
> And buzzing with the yellow bee.
> We'll swing you on the cedar bough,
>   Luriana, Lurilee.

I wonder if it seems to you,
   Luriana, Lurilee,
That all the lives we ever lived
And all the lives to be,
Are full of trees and changing leaves,
   Luriana, Lurilee.

How long it seems since you and I,
   Luriana, Lurilee,
Roamed in the forest where our kind
Had just begun to be,
And laughed and chattered in the flowers,
Luriana, Lurilee.

How long since you and I went out,
   Luriana, Lurilee,
To see the Kings go riding by
Over lawn and daisy lea,
With their palm leaves and cedar sheaves,
   Luriana, Lurilee.

Swing, swing on the cedar bough,
   Luriana, Lurilee,
Till you sleep in a bramble heap
Or under the gloomy churchyard tree,
And then fly back to swing on a bough,
   Luriana, Lurilee.

NOTES ON ENGLISH LITERATURE

Chief Adviser JOHN D. JUMP, *Professor of English Literature in the University of Manchester*

General Editor W. H. MASON, *Formerly Senior English Master, The Manchester Grammar School*

1 Shakespeare **Macbeth**
  JOHN HARVEY

2 Chaucer **The Prologue**
  R. W. V. ELLIOTT, *Professor of English, Flinders University, South Australia*

3 T. S. Eliot **Murder in the Cathedral**
  W. H. MASON

4 Austen **Pride and Prejudice**
  J. DALGLISH, *Sometime Senior English Master, Tiffin School*

5 Shakespeare **Twelfth Night**
  BARBARA HARDY, *Professor of English, Royal Holloway College*

7 Emily Brontë **Wuthering Heights**
  BARBARA HARDY

8 Hardy **The Mayor of Casterbridge**
  G. G. URWIN, *Senior English Master, Sale Grammar School for Boys*

9 Charlotte Brontë **Jane Eyre**
  BARBARA HARDY

10 Shaw **St. Joan**
  W. H. MASON

11 Conrad **Nostromo**
  C. B. COX, *Professor of English Literature, University of Manchester*

12 Dryden **Absalom and Achitophel**
W. GRAHAM, *Sometime Senior English Master, Dame Allan's Boys' School, Newcastle-upon-Tyne*

13 Sheridan **The Rivals, The School for Scandal, The Critic**
B. A. PHYTHIAN, *Senior English Master, The Manchester Grammar School*

14 Shakespeare **King Lear**
HELEN MORRIS, *Principal Lecturer in English, Homerton College, Cambridge*

15 Forster **A Passage to India**
W. H. MASON

16 Chaucer **The Nun's Priest's Tale and The Pardoner's Tale**
R. W. V. ELLIOTT

17 Milton **Paradise Lost, Books IV and IX**
W. GRAHAM

18 Shakespeare **King Richard II**
HELEN MORRIS

19 Browning **Men and Women**
MARK ROBERTS, *Professor of English Literature, Queen's University, Belfast*

20 Webster **The White Devil, The Duchess of Malfi**
JOHN D. JUMP, *Professor of English Literature, University of Manchester*

21 George Eliot **Middlemarch**
A. O. J. COCKSHUT, *Fellow of Hertford College, Oxford*

22 Shakespeare **The Winter's Tale**
G. FOX, *Assistant Master, The Manchester Grammar School*

23 Lawrence **Sons and Lovers**
CHRISTOPHER HANSON, *Lecturer in English Literature, University of Manchester*

24 Mrs. Gaskell   **Sylvia's Lovers**
GRAHAM HANDLEY, *Senior Lecturer in English, All Saints' College, Tottenham*

25 Shakespeare   **Antony & Cleopatra**
HELEN MORRIS

26 Wordsworth   **The Prelude I & II**
W. GRAHAM

27 Forster   **Howards End**
G. P. WAKEFIELD, *Senior English Master, King George V School, Southport*

28 Austen   **Persuasion**
J. R. COATES, *Senior English Master, Hymer's College, Kingston-upon-Hull*

29 Woolf   **To the Lighthouse**
W. A. DAVENPORT, *Lecturer in English, Royal Holloway College*

30 Shaw   **Man and Superman**
A. W. ENGLAND, *Senior Lecturer in English, Eaton Hall College of Education, Notts.*

31 Synge   **Playboy of the Western World, Riders to the Sea**
A. PRICE, *Senior Lecturer in Education, Queen's University, Belfast*

32 Byron   **Childe Harold III and IV, Vision of Judgement**
PATRICIA BALL, *Department of Literature, Royal Holloway College*

33 Shakespeare   **Othello**
G. P. WAKEFIELD

34 Dickens   **Bleak House**
P. DANIEL, *Ratcliffe College, Leicester*

35 Dickens   **Hard Times**
W. GRAHAM